INTERIM MINISTRY IN ACTION

INTERIM MINISTRY IN ACTION

A Handbook for Churches in Transition

Norman B. Bendroth

An Alban Institute Book

ROWMAN & LITTLEFIELD
Lanham • Boulder • New York • London

Published by Rowman & Littlefield
An imprint of The Rowman & Littlefield Publishing Group, Inc.
4501 Forbes Boulevard, Suite 200, Lanham, Maryland 20706
https://rowman.com

Unit A, Whitacre Mews, 26-34 Stannary Street, London SE11 4AB,
United Kingdom

British Library Cataloguing in Publication Information Available

Library of Congress Cataloging-in-Publication Data
Names: Bendroth, Norman B., author.
Title: Interim ministry in action : a handbook for churches in transition /
    Norman B. Bendroth.
Description: Lanham : Rowman & Littlefield, 2018. | "An Alban Institute
    book." | Includes bibliographical references and index.
Identifiers: LCCN 2018003734 (print) | LCCN 2018011354 (ebook) | ISBN
    9781538105009 (electronic) | ISBN 9781538104989 (cloth : alk. paper) |
    ISBN 9781538104996 (pbk. : alk. paper)
Subjects: LCSH: Interim clergy. | Change—Religious aspects—Christianity.
Classification: LCC BV676.3 (ebook) | LCC BV676.3 .B46 2018 (print) | DDC
    253—dc23
LC record available at https://lccn.loc.gov/2018003734

Printed in the United States of America

To Nathan, Anna, and Tamas
Who keep me honest, crazy, laughing, and faithful

CONTENTS

ACKNOWLEDGMENTS

When you finish writing a book you know you didn't do it alone. I'm in debt to local coffee shop owners and servers who wondered when I would leave.

I want to thank my colleagues who encouraged me to write this book when I told them of my idea. I particularly thank colleagues and friends David Sawyer, Ineke Mitchell, and John Keydel who read the first draft and shared helpful comments and suggestions.

Beth Gaede, my editor, always saves me from dangling participles, unaccounted-for pronouns, and pesky rabbit holes. I appreciate her direct but always kind edits.

I am grateful for Sarah Stanton's backing and belief in this project from the outset. Her patience and continuing encouragement when I missed yet another deadline was always appreciated.

And, of course, Peggy, my fellow traveler, best friend, and cheerleader. As an accomplished scholar in American religious history, she always has the perfect blend of cynicism and wise counsel about the churchy things I write.

As I write I am surrounded by two grand dogs who are thoroughly entertaining and two cats who take turns walking across my keyboard. My adult children, who have returned home (the new normal), and a new son-in-law make the mix of life, work, and love delightful.

INTRODUCTION

The fact that you have this book in your hands indicates that your church is going through some kind of transition. It could be that your beloved pastor of twenty-one years has announced her retirement. People are still reeling, wondering how they will make the adjustment.

It's also possible that you had a good run with your pastor and after nine years of fine work together, he has taken another call. While you will miss him, you are in good shape. Relationships are healthy, programs are well attended, people's lives are being changed, and you have a surplus in the bank. You're ready to go.

Or it could be that your pastor left under a cloud due to an intractable conflict, pastoral misconduct, or a mismatch. Some of the congregation liked him very much and others just couldn't stand him.

Your congregation may have had a serious kerfuffle over different worship styles, same-gender marriage, a pastor or staff member, or a building project. You still need help to work through the differences and come to some kind of resolution.

You might be facing the reality that your church is in survival mode, unable to meet the budget, fill boards and committees, or keep up with repairs on the building. People despair over how much longer you can keep it up. You know you can't keep doing the same thing over and over. You need some guidance!

If any of these descriptions fit your congregation, congratulations! You are in transition. Transitions are especially hard because you are in that in-between time. I have a therapist friend who says that most psychological problems come from places that don't exist: the past and the future. When we dwell on the past it can evoke feelings of nostalgia, regret, what-ifs, joy, and remorse. When we dwell on the future it can generate feelings of worry and dread or anticipation and excitement. The only time we have to live in is the present. We can and should learn from the past and prepare for and anticipate the future, but we don't have any control over either. We can only live in the present and make the most of it. This in-between time can be nerve-wracking and unsettling. It is much like a trapeze artist performing in the big top. She swings across the chasm, lets go of the bar, and is hanging in midair. She knows that there is another bar or trapeze artist heading her way, but it is a matter of trust.

All of these reasons are indicators that your church needs an intentional interim minister to guide you through the transition. The interim will help you discover who you are, your core values, and your purpose, mission, and vision, among other tasks. This process will enable you to be well prepared when you are ready to call a settled pastor. This book is intended to be a guidebook for calling an effective interim pastor and to inform about what you can expect.

The late William Bridges, in his book *Managing Transitions*, says that it is not change people have difficulty with, but it is transition from one place to another. Change is "situational." It is an external event. Something significant happens such as selling your family home of forty-seven years, leaving for college, or the departure of your pastor. Transition, says Bridges, is "psychological; it is a three phase process that people go through as they internalize and come to terms with the details of the new situation that the change brings about."[1] "Getting people through the transition," he continues, "is essential if the change is actually to work as planned."[2]

We all experience change in our lives, whether at work, at church, or in our families. Over the course of our lifetime we transition from being a toddler dependent upon mom, to first grade, middle school, high school, and college. We are hired for our first job, fall in love and get married, buy a house and have children. We see our children grow, get married, and have their children. We retire, grow old, and die. Life is perpetual change and people expect it. Change in a congregation, for instance, might be getting rid of a hymnal that has been used for years. There is grief because of the familiarity and comfort it brought to many worshippers. Transition is getting used to the new hymnal, appreciating many new songs, while being glad some of the old favorites remain.

Transition can be an emotional roller coaster and people deal with it differently. Some might find it to be a frightening, unsettling time, and they want someone to put them out of their pain as soon as possible. These folks may want to ramp up the search process rapidly so everything can "get back to normal." They may argue, "At my company when we need to fill a position, we hire a headhunter, do a nationwide search, and have someone in place in three months."

But churches aren't businesses or organizations, per se. Yes, they need to be business-like in running the institutional church by making budgets, raising money, having organizational structure and a set of policies and procedures. Yet the church is different. It is an organism, the "body of Christ," as Paul puts it (1 Corinthians 12:12, 27; Romans 12:4–5). It is made up of people, programs, and possibilities. It holds dreams, hopes, memories, and the story of God transforming lives over the decades.

Other members are paralyzed by the change and transition. They might pretend it's not happening and put on a happy or stoic face instead of acknowledging difficult feelings. Others may drag their feet as the process of self-study and searching for a new pastor begins. They may grow attached to the interim pastor and know that it will be hard to say goodbye to him or her, so they aren't eager to have the search move too quickly.

Still others find the transition an exciting opportunity. Things have gotten stale. They loved the previous pastor, but feel the church needs new leadership and innovative ideas. The pain of the first two groups of people is real and must be acknowledged and healed. They are not necessarily "wrong," but process emotions differently. For this third group, the transition is time to take stock, reflect on who we are and what God is calling the church to do and to be. This is why you need an interim pastor to help negotiate all these difficult feelings and to keep a steady hand on the till as you sail through choppy waters.

By now you may be asking what the difference between interim ministry and transitional ministry is. Transitional ministry is the umbrella under which a host of specialties reside. There are ministers who specialize in conflict management, clergy betrayal, helping a congregation end its ministry and close its doors, or helping a church engage in an intentional renewal program, to name a few. Intentional interim ministry is another subset of transitional ministry by a minister who specializes in helping a congregation transition from one pastor to another.

THE ROOTS OF INTERIM MINISTRY

The idea of interim ministry germinated in the late 1960s and early 1970s. Loren Mead, executive director of the Alban Institute (now a ministry at Duke Divinity School), and his colleagues conducted and published a study titled "The Interim Pastor: A Neglected Role in Parish Development."[3] In his research among churches in transition, Mead found that the in-between time was one of the most fruitful times for congregational development. Up until that time the practice was to hire a seasoned retired pastor during the search process to "hold hands" and "water the plants." Instead of doing that, Mead argued, pastors should make the most of this strategic opportunity for growth and reflection in churches.

Alban began to assemble a team to study the question further. The result was a model of change revolving around a series of developmental tasks of interim ministry: coming to terms with history, discovering a new identity, negotiating shifts of power and leadership, rethinking denominational linkages, and committing to new leadership and a new future. These developmental tasks have now been replaced with five focus points discussed in chapter 5 based upon new research and the experience of interim ministers and churches over decades of practice.

Based upon these initial studies, a fledgling organization called the Interim Ministry Network (IMN) was spun off from the Alban Institute in 1981. It was dedicated to training and credentialing those who would be intentional interim ministers. Today IMN is a professional organization with a membership of over thirteen hundred Christian and Jewish clergy from twenty-five denominations across the nation. They provide training, referrals, publications, and consulting, and set professional standards.

I have been a transitional minister for twenty-five years, having served in two settled positions and ten interim positions. I have interviewed for interim positions at double that number. In almost every instance, even when a judicatory official has well prepared a board or interim search committee in what they can expect during a transitional time, I have found that people are still bewildered about why they need an interim minister. There are many questions in their minds: What will she do? What should we expect? Will there be a lot of changes? What will we do? Why is all this self-study necessary? How long will he be here?

This book was written to address many of those questions and to allay the fears a congregation may have. As the subtitle, "A Handbook for Churches in Transition," suggests, this book is a guidebook for a board, interim search committee, or transition team to educate themselves about the process. Questions at the end of the chapters and exercises at the end of the book are meant to provoke discussion and prepare the leaders of the congregation for this stage in the life of your church. They, in turn, having received instruction, will be able to lead the congregation more effectively through the process.

A note about terminology: I've tried to be as generic as possible when talking about leadership in the local church and judicatory leadership in a denomination. Please plug in the title that is appropriate for your setting and denomination. You might have a board chair, warden, moderator, deacon, or elder. You could have a board, vestry, or session. Your ecclesiastical organization might be a diocese, conference, association, or region. Judicatory staff could be a bishop, associate conference minister, or superintendent—whatever the polity and organizational structure of your church and denomination. The principles and practices of this book are meant to be transferable.

The chapters can easily be read as stand-alone chapters or used as a reference during the interim time. The first chapter, "It's Not Your Parents' Church Anymore," discusses the whirlwind of changes we have seen in our culture, our churches, and the mission of the church in the past three to four decades. We need to know our new context to call a new pastor who has the gifts and the skills to help us do ministry in our unique setting.

We will then explore the nature of interim/transitional ministry in a chapter called "What Is Interim Ministry?" We'll look deeper at the nature and practice of this specialized ministry and what to expect. The next chapter, "Why Do We Need a Transitional Minister?," will make the case for having an interim minister in times of transition, followed by a chapter called "Who Should We Hire?" It's important to know the training, skills, and type of experience that is needed to be an effective interim minister. In addition, I talk about assessing the candidate and looking at the nuts and bolts of contracting and developing a job description.

The next chapter answers that question, "What Will We Do?" explaining the activities, conversations, and data that will be collected during the time together. Those in leadership as well as the entire congregation will want to know what they and the interim pastor will do together during the transition. There are five focus points that guide the process: heritage, leadership, mission, connections, and future; these will be explored in detail in that chapter. All of these chapters are ideally meant to be read before you begin your search for an interim pastor.

Fear of change can short-circuit the benefits of using the transitional time well, so the chapter called "But We Like Things the Way They Are" will demonstrate that change for change's sake is never the intent of the interim minister, but this is a time to experiment and reflect upon trying new things or doing familiar things better. The goal of this chapter is to lessen any anxiety that might be present in the congregation and provide assurance about the positive benefits of having an interim minister. The next chapter looks at the role of the interim minister—as a "Shepherd, Coach, Consultant, or Cheerleader," or all four.

The next chapter, "Like a Shark: Move Forward or Die," takes a hard-nosed look at the need to "do church" differently in the twenty-first century and how we might do so. Revitalization, renewal, or redevelopment are tasks a church may wish to explore and embrace during an interim time. Lastly, is "Ready, Set, Go," a chapter on preparing for the new pastor to make his or her entrance as smooth and healthy as possible.

In all of this, rest assured, this is not simply a one-size-fits-all template that an interim pastor uses on every church. He or she does not have a cookie-cutter approach, but recognizes that each church has a unique history and ways of doing things that are precious and need to be honored. Nor are these a set of sociological tools that treat a church just like any other social organization or nonprofit. My conviction is that the Holy Spirit is behind all our labors working quietly and inexorably. We are not simply going through the motions to find a new pastor but are seeking the mind of Christ and discerning together how the wind of the Spirit is blowing and guiding the ship that is our church.

The principles I follow are deeply rooted in the scriptures, particularly using the model of Moses leading the Israelites through the wilderness and passing the mantel of leadership to Joshua after his work was done (Joshua 1: 1–18). On the eve of his death, Moses asked God to provide a successor to lead the people into the Promised Land (Numbers 27: 16–17). Throughout Exodus and Numbers we see how God was preparing Joshua as Moses mentored him. In the same way, the interim pastor is preparing the way for a new leader even as the congregation is praying that God would raise up and reveal to them the pastoral leader they need for the next chapter in their story.

The church visible and invisible is the people of God called to model a lifestyle of love, service, and joy. We are embraced, loved, and forgiven by a merciful God. As Peter tells us, we are "a chosen race, a holy nation, God's own people . . . who called you out of darkness into his marvelous light" (1 Peter 2: 9–10). Yet God loves us too much to leave us as we are. We are called to personal transformation as Christ lives in and through us, and consequently, sends us to be transformers in the world in word and deed.

My prayer is that this book will be a strong and steady companion as you walk through your time of transition, using the time well, not resisting the process, embracing the possibilities, and finding Jesus Christ to be faithful in all your undertakings.

I

IT'S NOT YOUR PARENTS' CHURCH ANYMORE

A number of years ago General Motors tried to market Oldsmobile to a younger generation to boost their sagging sales and overcome the perception that an Olds was an old man's car. After showing off a sporty new model, the background voice pronounced, "It's not your father's Oldsmobile." Unfortunately, the strategy didn't work, and the once stolid Oldsmobile was dropped from GM's line. Many mainline churches find themselves in the same situation. The church today is not the one they grew up in. Stalwart members can't understand why people don't want to come to their church anymore. They need to realize that "It's not your parents' church anymore."

I, for instance, was born in 1953, and my parents bought their first home in 1955. It was a little Cape Cod–style house on a cul de sac in a brand-new, postwar, baby boom neighborhood. New families and kids were in abundant supply. I walked to the nearby elementary school, and we all worshiped at a local mainline church. It was a shiny new facility served by a handsome young minister with a wife and 2.5 kids. The place was packed with two Sunday morning services, Sunday school classes for all, and a huge youth group. Today the congregation is barely hanging on by its fingernails.

What happened? There have been three significant shifts in the past four to five decades: the culture has changed, the church has changed, and the mission has changed.

THE CULTURE HAS CHANGED

Our world is changing at a breakneck pace. Our taxes are done in India. McDonald's orders are taken two states away. A Microsoft customer service agent speaks to us from the Philippines. Every time we purchase or even look at something online, ads for the product pop up in our email and Facebook accounts. We have fresh fruits and vegetables shipped year-round from all over the world. As Thomas Friedman put it, "the world is flat."

Churches have either embraced the changes wholeheartedly, dug in their heels and resisted, or adapted as appropriate, yet our local churches and denominations continue to shrink in members and dollars. What's going on? Let me suggest seven (and there are many more) shifts in our culture over the past four decades that contribute to the changing religious landscape in America and impact how our churches function and how the population sees them.

1. Simple shifts in demographics changes the church's populations. Since 1991, for instance, the adult population in the United States grew by 15 percent. During that same period the unchurched population grew by 92 percent! Part of the reality is that all mainline churches are aging (as are evangelical churches, but not as much). The median age of adults in all mainline churches is fifty-two and churches have a disproportionate number of members age sixty-five and older. This reality will only grow more pronounced as eight thousand baby boomers will turn sixty-five every day for another sixteen years. While the younger cohort equals 65 percent of the population, they are only on average about 30 percent of existing congregations. The birthrate of mainline Protestants is also much lower so that the next generation is not filling the pews.[1]

There have also been major population shifts. A majority of the population has moved to metropolitan areas and large percentages have migrated to the South and the coasts. In 1960, those living in rural regions and in metropolitan areas was split fifty-fifty. By 2013, 20 percent of Americans lived in rural areas and 80 percent lived in metropolitan ones. The reality is that a large number of people have moved away from existing congregations.

2. American civil religion no longer supports churches. The postwar boom of church attendance was a fluke. Church attendance in

America was never that high before. There was prosperity and optimism after the war that was palpable. The GI bill enabled many returning soldiers to get a college degree and a good job. Young couples bought new homes and cars and settled into building a new middle class life. Church attendance was an expectation and there was a subtle social pressure to attend, unlike today. Christianity was confused or fused with American civil culture so that loyalty to God and country were almost synonymous. Communism was on the rise, compelling politicians to put "In God We Trust" on our currency and to insert "one nation, under God, indivisible" into the Pledge of Allegiance. Americans, unlike godless communists, believed in God and went to church.

The term "American civil religion" was coined by sociologist Robert Bellah to describe the set of rituals, doctrines, and beliefs that becomes the glue that holds a nation and its citizens together.[2] Historians have pointed out that American mythology tracks that of the biblical story. For instance, America's book of Genesis is the Mayflower Compact. Its exodus is the Declaration of Independence. The book of law is the Constitution and the Bill of Rights. Its Psalms include "The Star-Spangled Banner" and "God Bless America." Lincoln's Second Inaugural address is its prophetic denouncement.

Rituals include saying the Pledge of Allegiance before school begins in the morning, singing "The Star-Spangled Banner" at sporting events, having parades and ceremonies honoring the war dead, and invoking the blessing of some higher power at political events. The virtues of democracy, individual liberty, the right to private property, family, free enterprise, and a commitment to faith are part of its doctrines. Faith in this system of thought is vague and undefined. Dwight Eisenhower once said, "This country was founded on faith and I don't care in what." What is one having faith in? Is it solid ground?

Civil religion and Christian religion can look deceptively similar, so much so that it is easy to merge the two into one, like many American churches do on patriotic holidays. Civil religion is not necessarily a bad thing; it is often the glue that holds societies together. Churches today need to be distinct from the dominant culture and offer an alternative to its values. If we don't look that different from the culture around us, what is compelling people to participate in a local church?

3. A whole new world has arrived, creating a heterogeneous culture. In 1955 sociologist Will Herberg could write a book describing religion in America as "Protestant, Catholic, Jew." Forty-six years later Diana Eck of Harvard would write a book titled "A New Religious America: How a 'Christian Country' Has Become the World's Most Religiously Diverse Nation."[3] As the twenty-first century begins, we are just starting to grasp the implications of these realities. With the exception of some rural areas of our nation, the diversity of our population has exploded.

My daughter, who is Amerasian, graduated from a large urban high school where thirty-two different language groups were represented. There are more practicing Muslims in the United States today than Episcopalians and United Church of Christ members combined.[4] More people of African descent live in America than in any country except Nigeria, and there are almost as many Cubans living in Miami as there are in Havana.[5]

Many of our churches are ill-equipped to accommodate this ethnic and religious diversity. When people, especially young people or the unchurched, are exposed to such different worldviews and cultural values, they want to know what makes us different. All-white churches will also want to know how to adapt when the United States becomes a "minority majority" nation by 2060. This forces our churches to ask: What do we believe? What is distinctive about our faith? What is the meaning behind our rituals and traditions? How are we to participate in our communities? While wanting to be open and accepting of other faiths, what is the content of our own? Churches in transition must address these new questions.

4. Who's in charge? The crisis of authority has weakened trust in the church. The traditional sources of authority that held our society together are no longer particularly strong or shared. Doctors, lawyers, clergy, police, politicians, and judges were trusted leaders in our communities, but that trust has dropped precipitously. The 2008 market crash shook our faith in the economy and corporate America. The divisiveness and lack of civil discourse in the election of 2016 has given many pause about the state of our democracy. Major hacking of Experian and major corporations, gaining access to our most personal data, makes us wonder how secure we actually are.

Gallup reports that Americans' confidence in fourteen historically important institutions is at a record low. These include institutions such as the economy, politics, religion, and the media. Americans have lost confidence in ten of those fourteen institutions since 2006. The number of Americans expressing "a great deal" or "quite a lot" of confidence in the fourteen institutions is at only 33 percent. Newspapers and organized religion took the biggest hit, dropping to 11 percent and 10 percent respectively in the past decade.[6]

All of the institutions that had given us stability have unraveled. Consequently, people are not turning to the church for moral guidance, as a source of truth, or as a trustworthy institution; the same is true for every other institution in our society.

5. More and more people are calling themselves spiritual, but not religious. When polltakers survey the religious attitudes and beliefs of Americans, a whole new category called "Nones" has emerged. Sixteen percent of the population identify themselves as such. These are folks who don't identify with any particular religious tradition or denomination. Only a small percentage define themselves as atheists or agnostics (6 percent). Most are simply indifferent or were not raised in any religious tradition. They are largely millennials, those who are in their twenties and thirties. Surveys of religious belief in the 1960s consistently found that approximately 95 percent of Americans were certain that God existed. By 2014, that number was down to 63 percent.[7]

Belief systems have changed as well. In a 1999 Gallup Poll asking whether respondents understood themselves as spiritual or religious, 30 percent said spiritual only; 54 percent, religious only.[8] By 2014, the Pew Research Center's Forum on Religion & Public Life found that 49 percent of the adults who describe themselves as "unaffiliated" say they believe in God, 47 percent say that at least once a week they feel a sense of wonder about the universe, 27 percent say they think of themselves as "spiritual but not religious," up 8 percentage points from 2012, and 20 percent say they pray every day. What this tells us is that people are still hungry for a transcendent, spiritual, or religious experience, but they don't look to the institutional church to provide that.[9]

In her study of millennials (those born after 1980), Elizabeth Drescher, professor of Religion and Pastoral Ministries at Santa Clara University, found that young adults in this category found spirituality through family, Fido (animal companions), friends, nature, and prayer.

She surveyed those who claimed some kind of religious identity and asked how they connected with the Divine. Their answers were the same: family, Fido, friends, nature, and prayer.[10] Both groups experience God in similar ways, which makes one wonder why that didn't happen in church.

While traditional ways of experiencing God—worship, prayer, Bible study, small groups, service projects—are real, valid, and necessary, young adults in particular want a spirituality that grounds and connects them to the transcendent but find traditional or organized religion unable or unwilling to meet that need.

6. People view the world with a new set of glasses. A worldview is the set of values, assumptions, philosophies, convictions, experiences, and understandings that color how one interprets life and all its meanings. These would include things like gender roles, how to raise children, the role of government, how to dress on special occasions, why people are poor, how to spend money, why there is something rather than nothing, and what constitutes moral and ethical behavior.

Back in the 1950s and 1960s when our country was more homogenous there was a shared set of values: the virtues of democracy, individual liberty, the right to private property, family, free enterprise, a commitment to faith, hard work, and thrift, the relationship of races, the appropriate role of men and women, and proper heterosexual behavior were part of the lexicon of virtues and mutual understanding.

All that changed as the civil rights movement and the women's movement challenged social arrangements that had been in place for generations. The war in Vietnam pitted fathers and sons against one another, the divorce rate began rising to 50 percent, and contraceptives gave women unprecedented control of their lives.

What we now know is that the experience of men and women, gay and straight, rich and poor, people of different ethnicities, urban and rural, East Coast, West Coast, and Midwest, to name a few, are not universal. Our geography, social class, gender, sexual orientation, race, and nationality impact how we view reality. People see the world through different sets of glasses.

Urban African American young men view police with much more suspicion and threat than do their white peers in suburbia. Women view sexual harassment as a violation, whereas some men don't see it as a big deal. The poor see themselves as locked in a rigged system of closed doors and few choices, whereas the wealthy have only known prosperity and are clueless about the ravages of poverty. A North American Christian might read the Bible looking for comfort and guidance for personal relationships, whereas a Palestinian Christian will take hope in Mary's Magnificat claiming the promise that God will one day judge the oppressor and usher in justice and peace for the downtrodden.

The plethora of worldviews, never mind religious worldviews, is a challenge for churches that for generations had expectations and assumptions that are no longer shared. The Christian right and media have not done us any favors either, as surveys show that young adults perceive the Christian faith as politically right wing, antiscience, homophobic, judgmental, insensitive, exclusive, and dull.

7. We live in a post-Christian, postmodern world. Two more lenses by which our culture views the world are called postmodern and post-Christian. "Post" means after, which means that neither modern ways of thinking nor Christianity are dominant in how people understand the world. Modernity is the intellectual and cultural worldview of the Enlightenment. Enlightenment thinkers rejected traditional and religious sources of authority in favor of reason and knowledge. The benchmarks of modernity included a trust in reason, progress, technology, individualism, personal autonomy, and tolerance. Postmodernity challenges the notion that there is anything such as universal truth or one story that can speak for all of humanity. While there may be "ultimate" or "universal truth," it is very hard to grasp. No one has a "God's eye" view of the world.

Modernity operates under the assumption that the world is essentially linear. If there is an effect, there must be a cause. If there is a problem, you find the cause and fix it. The world works mechanistically, like a machine with moving parts and predictable behavior. If a part is broken, you replace it. It functions on the belief that human beings have the ability to plan, achieve progress, and solve problems using science and technology. There is nothing wrong with this worldview. After all it gave us automobiles, air travel, and central heat and air conditioning in our homes, and it is still the basis of our technological and engineering advances.

Postmodernity, however, is characterized by a loss of faith in science and rationality as the *only* source of knowledge and truth, a loss of belief in progress, and increased skepticism about any theory that claims to be able to produce a better future. Postmodernity sees the world systemically with an interconnection of many pieces, influences, and forces. This is why the internet is called the "worldwide web." We understand families and churches as "emotional systems," where a disruption in one part of the system has a ripple effect throughout the whole system.

Postmodernity is the worldview shaping baby boomers forward, even if they are not consciously aware of it. There is no longer a binding story of how America or the world works. They lack confidence in the institutions that sustained previous generations and are suspicious of trite answers. iPhones, Facebook, Twitter, Snapchat, and reality TV inform their worldview, providing overwhelming choices and an exposure to a mountain of information. This creates a world that is in perpetual motion with no center of gravity.

Postmodernity should not be viewed as a bad thing. If anything, it expands our horizons as we see that the principles of biology, cosmology, and psychology are operative in many spheres of our lives. The whole is greater than the sum of the parts. We can hold our "truths" with our hands more open knowing that, as St. Paul puts it, "we now see in a mirror darkly."

Post-Christian is the reality that the United States can no longer be called a "Christian" nation, if it ever was one. We are at the end of an era. The age of Christendom, when Christianity was the establishment religion of America, is gone. In a post-Christian age, there is not a shared worldview. Christians are but one player in the marketplace of ideas.

There are a number of significant ways living in a post-Christian and postmodern world has impacted the church. First, many newcomers to our church have only a peripheral knowledge and superficial understanding of the Christian faith. They have not been raised in a world where Judeo-Christian values to a large extent shaped society. The teachings and practices of Christianity are foreign to them.

Second, truth is subjective and relative, largely internal and personal. Truth is what's true for me. There is no "objective" reality that all share. While we as Christians may acknowledge there is objective reality found in God, we also know that we can't grasp it in its entirety because we don't have God's view. Postmoderns often don't find an overarching meaning or purpose to the universe such as Christianity.

Third, a post-Christian and postmodern worldview impacts ethics and moral decision making. These too are seated in the subjective self. We see this in attitudes toward the body and sexuality. If we do not see ourselves made in the image of God or temples of the Holy Spirit, and we are simply part of the animal kingdom, our humanity is diminished and our behavior is not governed by a thoughtful set of values.

Fourth, practically speaking, when a newcomer shaped by these worldviews visits our worship services they will find bulletins, hymnals, newsletters, and prayer books. This is all printed material that is largely absorbed by the brain (neck up, if you will). Most young adults get their information on the web saturated with images, experiences, and an overflow of incoming data. Consequently, our worship has little or no appeal because it isn't multisensory. Worship that can be experienced through sight, sound, smell, touch, and movement is most moving and meaningful.

Lastly, relationships are more important than correct beliefs or behavior. Often, as young adults or seekers are immersed in the life of a congregation they begin to behave differently, by beginning to pray, working on service projects, attending adult education classes, and reading the Bible. They then begin to believe, as they experience the Holy in a loving Christian community. In their monumental study of religious belief and practice in the United States, sociologists Robert Putnam and David Campbell found that being part of a community was the most compelling reason for being part of a faith community, even more so than worship or religious instruction. [11]

What many in our society have been exposed to is what Quaker Elton Trueblood called "cut flower" Christianity. People can hold the values of Christianity, such as the Golden Rule, but they are not rooted in the soil of an abiding faith in Christ.

Philosopher and theologian Peter Kreeft captures well the condition of our day. "Our culture," he writes, "has filled our heads but emptied our hearts, stuffed our wallets but starved our wonder. It has fed our thirst for facts but not for meaning or mystery. It produces 'nice' people, not heroes." [12]

THE CHURCH HAS CHANGED

Quite a few years ago I served a church that I will simply call "that which shall not be named." The search committee was representative of this old, crusty Yankee congregation with its venerated history, tall white steeple, and "Founded in 1638" emblazoned on its bulletin cover every week. The previous pastor had been there for eighteen years and, by the admission of the search committee, had coasted into retirement. "We need someone to shake us up," they said. "Someone with fresh ideas who can bring young people into the church." I was up for a challenge, so I took the job. The tacit assumption was, "If we just hire a nice young minister with a young family, he'll attract new young people."

I started doing all the things that church growth folks said you should do—introduce contemporary elements into the worship, make sure you're visible with good signage and advertising, create small groups around the interests and demographics of the congregation, and so forth. Of course there was some rumbling, but then I really crossed the line. In an effort to have the bulletin cover match the theme of the day, the scripture, and the sermon, I took the picture of the church building off the cover and replaced it with—scripture! Otherwise stable women started having the vapors. Grown men openly wept. Dogs bayed at the moon.

I found out what I was up against one day while visiting a parishioner. After tea, cookies, and sharing niceties, she began questioning me. "Let me ask you, pastor, you wouldn't go into the Fairbanks House and rearrange the furniture, would you?" (The Fairbanks House is believed to be the oldest surviving timber frame house in North America. It was built for a family of Puritan immigrants from Yorkshire in England, Jonathan and Grace Fairebanks and their six children. Tree ring dating has confirmed a construction date of the late 1630s. This is not a house to be messed with.) "No," I said, "I would not." "Then why," she continued, "are you trying to change things in the church?"

I almost choked on my lemon-ginger scone; she was serious. I tried to explain that the Fairbanks House was a museum and the church was not, but she would have none of it. It became clear to me that for some the church was a sarcophagus, simply a place from which to be buried. In this woman's mind the church was an institution, an organization that largely exists for members who pay their dues (annual pledge) and in return receive religious goods and services (baptisms, weddings, and funerals).

I have a friend who led a church that was on its last leg to become a thriving, multicultural church offering dozens of ministries and programs. I asked what led to the turnaround. He told me, "I learned that business as usual, even done well, no longer works." Our historic, mainline churches need to heed this observation as well as recover a biblical perspective on the purpose of the church. If we take Paul's analogy that the church (meaning the people) is the body of Christ, a living, breathing, growing, changing, adapting organism, then the church can't remain the same. To repeat: we are an organism not an organization. And to those who would say, "I don't like organized religion," I would say, "Well, you should come visit us; we're not very organized at all." Churches whose purpose becomes to maintain an institution will not survive. But churches that learn to adapt to the changing religious landscape will find they will not only survive but thrive.

We'll now look at how the mission has changed and how to respond effectively. We will then return to how our churches need to respond to the new realities of our day to be effective.

THE MISSION HAS CHANGED

If you asked anyone in your church "Why do we exist?," you might get a blank look. Often it's because no one had ever asked before. "Of course, everyone knows why we exist. We are like family. We take care of one another. We have an excellent music program. We are known for our Sunday school and youth programming." "Yes, all true and good, but why do *we* exist?" We need to keep asking and asking and asking that question, peeling back the layers until we get to the kernel of the question. What is our reason for being? What makes us unique as a congregation? What is our reputation in the community? If we disappeared would anyone notice? What would they miss? If we're just a religious social club, why put so much money and effort in maintaining the institution when we could meet in people's homes and pray?

If, as noted above, the church needs to recover its purpose of transforming human lives in the name of Jesus Christ, it also needs to discover how to do mission in our day. For many years, mission was more likely to be referred to as "missions" and was done somewhere in Africa or Center City Philadelphia by a ministry of some kind and supported by congregations. Churches would (and do) send money to their denomination, the local food pantry or college ministry, or to a Christian school in the Philippines.

Yet the way mission is carried forward within the local church is changing. When people describe where God is most present in churches today, previous understandings of mission are not in mind. What has changed and how are churches responding? Lovett H. Weems, director of the Lewis Center for Church Leadership, names seven changes.[13]

Churches are doing much more work locally. Each year a large downtown church in Boston sets a goal to raise at least one more dollar for missions than the previous year. If they raised a million dollars last year, they would raise a million and one this year. And they did it! For years. But then something happened. Missions giving began to go down. Leaders wondered whether commitment was flagging, or was the church becoming more ingrown? Neither of these things were true. What was true is that younger generations wanted to focus more locally, on their neighborhoods, city, and community. It's not that these churches stopped having a national and global component, but that scope of missional engagement is more comprehensive.

People want more hands-on opportunities. Baby boomers and millennials tend to want to get their hands dirty. There is more of a personal connection and they can better see the fruits of their labor. Most annual reports contain long lists of agencies and ministries that corporations willingly give to year after year. That is rightly a source of pride and an indicator of good work being done. But today you're just as likely to see a list of mission projects to which people gave both money *and* time. You might see the monthly meal served at the shelter, the work being done on a Habitat for Humanity build, or collecting school bags for Church World Service. Still others have taken mission trips to Mexico, the Pine Ridge Reservation in South Dakota to work with the Lakota Sioux, or an inner city.

Mission is not done *for* someone, but *with* someone. Increasingly, mission is seen not as what you do *for* the community but what you do *with* the community. Mission that is paternalistic, as in we're here to help you, creates an "us" and "them" relationship instead of a partnership. As Jesse Jackson put it, "People don't want a hand out, but a hand up." People don't want to be treated as a "spiritual project," but as a child of God worthy of respect. Churches that come to see themselves as part of the community have a mutuality of giving and receiving that empowers and inspires those being helped and earns the good will of the community. Being in community with those who receive the gifts of mission—be it food, clothing, financial counseling, a home through Habitat for Humanity, or tutoring—creates relationships where all have the chance to experience the abundant life God desires. Building relationships, and not just carrying out tasks or writing checks, creates mission with integrity.

Partnerships and networks are important. In the past, churches largely did mission through denominational agencies or on their own. They had a list of agencies to which they had been writing checks for generations. Today there are networks of churches, nonprofits, and municipalities that often develop around a particular issue or need in a community about which people have a shared passion. In Boston, for instance, Protestant, Roman Catholic, Orthodox, Jewish, and Muslim communities have formed what is called the Greater Boston Interfaith Organization (GBIO).

GBIO's mission is to coalesce, train, and organize the communities of Greater Boston across religious, racial, ethnic, class, and neighborhood lines for the public good. Together they discern issues that impact their communities and give a voice to the voiceless. Since their founding in 1998 they have challenged city and state legislators, business leaders, and educational institutions to take action on criminal justice reform, gun violence, aging with dignity, health care reform, financial literacy, education, and affordable housing. Their success has been considerable. Here is but one example.

GBIO's efforts caused the Massachusetts state legislature to create a $100 million Affordable Housing Trust Fund, reversing a fifteen-year trend of taking money away from affordable housing. Through 2016, more than $313 million has been invested in the fund, providing over 17,700 units of affordable housing statewide.

They sponsor community events to press candidates when running for public office to make commitments that would assist low-income families. Churches are also teaming up to create local Habitat for Humanity chapters, after-school programs, or a Vacation Bible school. There is not much room for "lone rangers" these days.

Direct giving beyond denominational channels has increased. In the past, many churches gave through their denomination either for the general mission fund or for a specific project. Today a much larger percentage of congregational mission giving goes directly to an agency or program outside the denominiation. Congregations make direct contributions to the Heifer Project or the prison chaplaincy program likely because there is a relationship or some history with the organization. Giving tends to go to ministries about which parishioners are passionate.

Church property is seen as a ministry asset. Many churches have come to see their buildings as a place for mission, not just as a space for the congregation, and seek creative ways to use their property to serve their communities. Other churches wonder if additional "bricks and mortar" investments are the best ways to use funds. This does not mean they intend to defer necessary maintenance, but to think intentionally about how the church building can be used to enhance mission and to have an awareness of the impact on mission before acquiring more property. Many churches already have twelve-step programs meeting in their building or sponsor a preschool program. Others still have feeding programs, a drop-in center for the homeless, or even a shelter. Thinking outside of the box can produce creative results for touching human lives and build an awareness in the community that something significant is happening at your church.

Mission work can be a "side door" entry into the life of the church. While most new people come into the life of a church for Sunday morning worship, there is growing evidence to suggest that younger adults are often first attracted to hands-on projects churches may be offering. In other words, they come in through the side door instead of the front door. Vital, invitational mission can be a means of congregational growth as participants find that it is the love of God that compels them to serve others. Church-wide mission projects and trips are a great way to bring people together across generational, denominational, racial, and social lines.

HOW SHALL WE THEN LIVE?

We have taken a whirlwind trip pointing to sign posts along the way as to how our culture has changed, how the church has changed, and how the mission has changed. It is easy to point out probems and pitfalls, but our churches want direction on how to tackle these issues. What I present below is not a blueprint that guarantees successful outcomes, but a set of practices that each congregation needs to reflect upon to discern God's direction and begin taking steps suited to their unique setting and personality.

First, we must recover our reason for being. In the era of American Christendom, when Christianity was the unofficial official religion of North America, and when a half dozen mainline Protestant denominations were the religious establishment of the country, the purpose of the church was to support a "civic faith" or "civil religion." The role of the church was to be the conscience of the community, the instrument of aid, the center of community and family life, and the custodian of shared American values. In some ways, the church was "the Rotary Club at prayer." These are not necessarily bad things and they served a useful function in another era. In return for playing this useful role, the culture supported this religious ethos as long as it didn't challenge the status quo—until the civil rights movement and the war in Vietnam. So if someone asked, "Why does the church exist?" people would look at you cross-eyed; it was a dumb question.

Peter Drucker, the famed management guru and consultant to many of America's corporations, made a career out of asking three simple questions: "What business are you in?" "Who's your customer?" and "What does the customer value?" While we may grimace at the use of business language in relation to churches, Drucker's questions do apply to the church's ministry and mission.

- "What is our business?" Calling people to faith in Jesus Christ and shaping them into faithful disciples.
- "Who is the customer?" Church members and attendees, spiritual seekers, and the unchurched.
- "What does the customer value?" This is all over the map, including an experience with the living God, community, music and

worship, outlets for ministry, and so on; but if we plan everything for insiders, we will never attract outsiders.

After Drucker asked, "What business are you in?" he would always follow up with "How's business?"[14]

In our culture today, the church is no longer the center of the community. We live in a multicentered world and most people's lives are lived amid multiple loyalties. The school is one center, work another, town government, sports, the mall, clubs or nonprofits still others. The church is one subset of all those other centers of allegiance and activity. The purpose of the church today, much more in keeping with the church as laid out in the New Testament and in a pre-Christendom era, is to change lives by nurturing people in a life-changing relationship with the living God. Gone is the day when people come to the church as a way of being part of the community or being good citizens. We cannot expect newcomers to wander in simply because we open our doors. More often than not people come to church today because of a crisis— it might be the ordinary crisis of having a new child or it could be more serious like the suicide of a brother, the loss of a job, news of a cancerous growth, divorce, depression, a problem of substance abuse, or a tragedy such as 9/11 or the Boston Marathon bombing. People do not come to church for potlucks, a movie review from the pulpit, or to hear ten minutes of announcements for insiders. They come to worship for a transcendent encounter with the Holy, the Divine, the living God, however you might identify it.

They also come in through what I previously called side-door entries. These are ministries such as Habitat for Humanity, meals at a soup kitchen, or workshops on death and dying, where people do not come to worship through the front door, but come to participate in some ministry activity or offering where you enter through the side door. In these cases people are coming to make meaning in their lives and to make a difference in the world.

Second, we need to move from Christendom to a vitalized faith. The leading-edge question for people finding their way back to church today is "How can I have a spiritual life?" or "How can I get God into my life?" or "How can I be different?" To the extent that a church has become an organization or a club it cannot provide answers to those questions. Remember, Christendom is the idea that Christianity is the establishment religion of the United States, an institution that was part and parcel of the American Way.

One of the first steps toward revitalization and transformation is to admit that we need changing, or to put it in theological language, that we "need to be saved." That's a tough conclusion to draw when the slogan "I'm OK; you're OK" is in the air we breathe and the water we drink. We assume we don't need changing, saving, or God. Many believe that the highest duty and purpose in life is to be true to ourselves. Clearly, there is merit in being self-aware and following the maxim "to thine own self be true." We do need integrity; but the presumption that what we most need is to discover and be true to ourselves needs closer examination.

There is a doctrine of human nature here at work. The first is the secular doctrine of the autonomous individual who depends upon nothing but his or her inner resources. We are children of the Enlightenment—that school of thought that found religion and revelation to be superstitious and unenlightened. Our salvation was thought to be found in human reason, the scientific method, and independence. Descartes taught us "I think, therefore I am." Rousseau promoted the idea that the individual was complete, competent, and good by nature and that we are corrupted by social conventions, our families, and dangerous dogma. This doctrine of human nature encourages self-deception rather than honesty. It locates the totality of reality deep within and it bends everything to one criterion: "Does this work for me?" and not "Is it true?" or "Is it right?"

From a Christian point of view, this is taking ourselves way too seriously. We have quite a different view of human nature. We are not alone; we are not autonomous human individuals answerable only to ourselves. We belong to God and are dependent upon God. There is an Other: a power and a reality beyond ourselves upon whom we can rely, in whom we can trust, to whom we are accountable. The gap between the brokenness of the world and the goodness of God is surely an indication that we are in need of formation and reformation in order to flourish. Where modern culture says that it is enough to follow our own lights, Christianity says that we are in need of a reformation of the self in order to master ourselves. We are called to resist those aspects of culture that distort our true self made in the image of Christ. This is the "saving" work that God in Jesus Christ must do for us. We are not good by nature and corrupted by society, as modernity has maintained; we are created good, but fallen and fundamentally flawed in need of constant renewal and restoration.

To put this more positively, Christianity offers the path of healing and transformation, but it is only through the path of surrender. Freedom is found by letting go; finding ourselves by dying to our old selves. Liberty is found in service to others. These, of course, are paradoxes—Gospel paradoxes. In contrast to a culture that teaches the more we are in "control" of ourselves the happier we will be, Christianity teaches that by surrendering ourselves to God, by seeing the illusions of control and autonomy for what they are, only then will we find true freedom and peace.

Third, we need to move from being a holy club to a mission outpost. The good people are not in here and the bad people out there. We are a fellowship, a gathering of those who are "being saved." We are on a journey, in the process of being changed, and we invite others to join us on this journey. Martin Luther used baptism to explain this process, which theologians call sanctification. While baptism is a once-in-a-lifetime experience, he explained, it takes a lifetime to complete.

Often the story of Nicodemus in John 3 is held up by Christians as a model of how to become a Christian. Under cover of darkness, Nicodemus, a Jewish rabbi, seeks out Jesus, curious about this young preacher and his growing following. He tried to engage Jesus in a theological discussion about what he was doing, kind of a Q & A session. Jesus shows no interest and says, "You must be born anew from above. You must be born again." "What are you talking about?" Nicodemus stammers. "I find religion fascinating, really. I could talk about it for hours. But I'm not up for a personal overhaul or any kind of new birth—whatever that is!"

This is called being "born again." It is a call to transformation, to redemption and renewal, but it is not a onetime experience. In my experience, I have been born again and again and again. We may have a powerful religious experience, epiphany, or conversion, but it never ends there, or at least it shouldn't. We have many conversions.

And there are many ways of coming to faith in the New Testament. Yes, Paul had a dramatic "Damascus Road" experience, but Timothy was raised as a Christian under the quiet influence of his Aunt Lois. Nicodemus may have been born again in a dramatic fashion, but Paul also tells the Thessalonians that he nursed them into the faith, loving them like a father.

Faith is a gift that needs to be continually nurtured and renewed. We may "get it," but we don't "have it." There was a campaign in the 1970s by the college ministry Campus Crusade for Christ called "I've Found It." That phrase was brandished on bright yellow posters and bumper stickers. When someone asked you, "What have you found?" you were supposed to reply, "New life in Jesus Christ" and share the Four Spiritual Laws with them. Catholics did them one better. They made up a bumper sticker that said, "We Never Lost It."

The point is faith is not a commodity that the church dispenses like soup in a bread line. Yes, we hold these treasures, this pearl of great price, and the riches of the faith—but not in a vault. It is a well that we invite all thirsty souls to drink from. In the past, mainline Protestants assumed they had the religious goods. We assumed that by virtue of being born and raised in the United States that you were a Christian and that you understood the basics of Christian faith and identity. But we weren't necessarily transforming lives. Rather we were baptizing the status quo.

The transformations we witness in our church and our lives may not be as dramatic as when German Christians rallied and helped bring down the Berlin Wall, for instance, but they are just as real. Ask the recovering alcoholic. Ask the abused woman who is living her life with dignity and hope instead of fear and despair. Ask the person who formerly spent his life focused on himself but is today working with homeless folks. As pastor, author, and church consultant Tony Robinson put it, we need to shift from assuming we've got the goods to sharing the goods with others.[15] In a real sense, only God can deliver the goods, but we've got to give God something to work with. If someone comes having a hunger in their heart or having just discovered Christ in a new and real way, one of the surest ways to kill that is to put them on a committee, assume they know the faith, and serve up a bland and moralistic religion that has little or no content. By "delivering the goods," I mean the church will pay attention to a few vital things, namely worship, teaching, and community. These are at the heart of Christian formation, how Christ is formed in us, and how the church "makes disciples."

In an earlier era, that would have shocked us. "What do you mean I need formation? Aren't I good enough the way I am? Aren't I kinda, sorta a Christian?" An adaptive church today needs to answer, no, you cannot be a Christian without formation, without ongoing learning, training, practice, and being in community with fellow travelers.

Fourth, we need to find new ways of "doing church." In his book *Transforming Congregational Culture*, Tony Robinson says that churches need to make strategic shifts from the old model of "doing church" to the new realities of the twenty-first century.[16] He contends that we must move from being givers to receivers who give, from a board culture to a ministry culture, from a community organization to a faith-based ministry, from democracy to discernment, from the budget as an end to the budget as a means to do ministry, from fellowship to hospitality, and from passive membership growth to active invitation. I think he's right. Let me comment on these.

Stewardship will no longer be about simply paying our fair share to support the church as an institution, keeping the doors open, the lights on, and the minister paid. Stewardship is about supporting the vision of the church, whether that vision includes vibrant worship, quality classes in Christian formation, or a "green" ministry that includes lowering the church's carbon footprint and helping the community to become more energy efficient. We give, not out of a sense of obligation, but from a heart filled with gratitude. We are fed by teaching, worship, small groups, and mission opportunities and then we take off our bibs, put on our aprons, and give back out of our fullness.

Similarly, a budget is not an end in itself but the means to do the ministry God has called the church to perform. Budgets are moral documents. If you want to know what is most important to an individual or a church, look at their bank account and their calendar. That will lay out their priorities in black and white. It was Jesus who said, "For wherever your treasure is, there your heart will be also" (Matthew 6: 21). Consider a zero sum budget where the church first decides what it thinks God is asking them to be and to do, and then asks for the money to support the mutual goals.

Many people feel that church life, especially in free church or congregational forms of government, is democracy at prayer. Each person has one vote, and the majority rules. Robert's Rules of Order wins the day and all is done decently and in order. The only trouble is there are winners and losers. There is an ancient practice that is being recovered called "discernment," whereby through scripture study, prayer, and listening to understand but not to win an argument, congregations invite God to speak to them. Instead of cooking up our own ideas and asking God to bless them, we listen to hear what God may be percolating within a given community of faith.

Too many church boards micromanage the work of committees and the staff instead of setting policy and making sure the church is on track to meet its goals and objectives. Or they become a reporting committee with no real power or authority, where each committee shares its minutes and activities and perhaps coordinates the calendar. The role of a board is to function as the fiduciary trustees of an organization. However, while boards provide a management role and are stewards of the assets of the organization, a church board plays a different role than that of a secular board. A board (or council, session, vestry) is to cast the vision of the church and to make sure the congregation is on task. Their role is to set policy and encourage excellence in the tasks of ministry found in Acts 2: 42–27, namely, worship, teaching, caregiving, stewardship, and mission. Boards at their best are "permission giving" agencies, rather than "permission getting" agencies, so that when people come with exciting and creative ideas for ministry they are encouraged to give it a try rather than dissuaded under an avalanche of objections and anxieties about everything that might go wrong.

Related to this, vibrant and growing churches focus less on "doing things to get people into the church" and instead look for ways to get into the community. To be sure, being known in the community as one of many churches or nonprofit agencies that do good things is positive, but to be known as a congregation that understands and meets the need of its neighbors in creative ways is even better. To be a "faith-based" or "Christ-centered" ministry is what distinguishes churches from the Lion's Club, Rotary, or any other service organization.

We often think of fellowship as sharing a cup of coffee and shooting the breeze with friends and fellow churchgoers after worship. But fellowship or *koinonia* as it is described in the New Testament goes deeper. It is a hospitality that welcomes the stranger and newcomer with open arms. Newcomers should be treated as VIPs, as guests and not as potential members. Hospitality cares for those within the congregation by having a system to stay in touch with the pastoral needs of its members. Hospitality is where people gather in one another's home to share a meal and have thoughtful conversation about what makes meaning in their lives. Hospitality is a camaraderie that goes deep and risks being transparent and vulnerable as we open and share our lives together. This is much more difficult for some than others. However, by providing small groups, whether Bible studies, book groups, spiritual practices groups, mission outreach groups, or common interest groups, these provide ways for people to go deeper in their relationship with God and one another.

Lastly, let's look at how we grow. Four to five decades ago, it was a given that each family would identify with or be part of some kind of religious community. When you moved to a new town you would register your kids for school, find a bank, a dentist, and a doctor, and begin looking for a church. You usually shopped by brand—Methodist, Baptist, Presbyterian, or Episcopalian. If one of those didn't fit, you'd find a similar church with a decent pastor and good Christian education. Simply by opening the doors of the church, the church would grow. Those days are long gone. We can call that unintentional church growth that almost happens by accident.

There is often no purposeful effort being made to regularly bring people into the church or any of its ministries. Many churchgoers respond, "Well, I don't want to be pushy or shove my religion down anyone's throat." I would agree if that is what we did. But most of us are so timid we won't even take the chance of telling the moms we meet at school or Girl Scouts that we and our kids have benefitted so much from the Sunday school at our church. What if you took a chance and posted on Facebook, "What an uplifting worship service we had today. The music was over the top!" You might be surprised who responds. The surveys I cited in the section above called "The Culture Has Changed" indicates that people have hungry hearts even if they aren't affiliated with a traditional church. A spiritual but not religious person might just respond positively if, after they shared what a tough patch of life they were going through, you told them you would pray for them.

There are scores of books and articles on church growth and vitality, new ways of being the church in our day, and how culture shapes our ministry, which are listed in the bibliography. Here I've just highlighted a few for you and your congregation to chew on.

Remember how I said that Peter Drucker would ask a business or nonprofit, "What's your business?" He always followed up the question with, "How's business?" How are we measuring success? By how many butts are in the pews and bucks in the offering plate, or by how lives are being changed? By a balanced budget or the new parenting class being offered at the library by our church? How has the mission changed in our day?

CONCLUSION

This chapter was meant to be a primer on the changing religious land-scape in the United States and how it impacts ministry today. It may not describe your church in every way, but I imagine it does in some of the ways I described. Maybe you've already begun to address the impact of a changing culture, church, and mission. If so, bravo! This is the water the church swims in today.

John Dorhauer, president and minister of the United Church of Christ, compares shifts in the church and culture to software upgrades. He speaks of church 1.0, 2.0, and 3.0.[17] Church 1.0 was the church before the Reformation, which started as a vibrant, new movement of Jesus's followers after his resurrection. Over the centuries the church became calcified and institutionalized. All authority rested in the church hierarcy and the "magisterium," the official teaching of the church. The Reformation was a protest of what the church had become. In Dorhauer's scheme it was church 2.0. The Reformers put the Bible and the ministry into the hands of the people and the church rose and fell with both glory and shame for the next five hundred years. Church 2.0 is what most churches in North America are using today and it has served us well.

But now we live in a new post-Christian, postmodern era that re-quires an update to church 3.0. This movement is called the Emerging Church because new ways of being the "body of Christ" are emerging. No one knows what it will look like. It is very much in flux and likely a variety of forms will appear with differing sources of authority, ways of training clergy and exercising leadership, gathering places besides church buildings, ways of doing worship and meeting human needs. It's a time of experimentation and excitement.

By his own admission, Dorhauer admits this analogy is not a particu-larly nuanced or sophistated approach to church history or culture, but it is a helpful, familiar parallel to understand what is going on in the ecclesiastical world.

Dorhauer is emphatic in saying that church 3.0 is not *replacing* church 2.0, but that it is something entirely different. Nor does he say that church 2.0 should try to mimic church 3.0 in order to be successful. That would likely fail. He asserts that church 2.0 is still a vital, viable way of "doing" and "being" church, but that something new is growing alongside it. This book is in fact for 2.0 churches, to help congregations become strong, healthy, and active communities of faith. Many 2.0 chuches may plant, support, or host a 3.0 church in their building, but 2.0 churches should not try to become something they are not. My purpose here is to introduce you to this new phenomenon of Christianty that is emerging and to encourage you to study, appreciate, and learn from it.

My intent in this chapter was not to discourage anyone, but to name the realties we face. To reframe it, these are exciting times to be the church. They present opportunities to be innovative, to listen and look for where the Holy Spirit is being active, and to experiment.

One job of the interim minister is to help the congregation to recognize and navigate the choppy waters of ministry today. We will next look at what exactly interim ministry is.

QUESTIONS FOR REFLECTION OR DISCUSSION

1. What struck you most about this chapter?
2. How have the shifts seen in culture and church shown up in your congregation?
3. How willing do you think people are to engage the transitional process and try doing church differently?

EXERCISE

Fold your hands together like you normally would. Now unfold them and refold them the opposite way (i.e., if your normal way is to have your left index finger on top of your right hand, refold your hands so it is one finger below). How does this change feel? What's odd about it?

How might this exercise apply to how we feel when new or unfamiliar things happen in our lives? How might it inform us about the "strangeness" or unfamiliarily when we start a new ministry with an interim pastor?

2

WHAT IS INTERIM MINISTRY?

It was the congregation's first Sunday with the freshly minted young minister. He had accepted his first call to Ida Baptist Church in the Northeast Kingdom of Vermont. As he was greeting people at the door after worship, a crusty old deacon came up to him and shook his hand. He informed the young minister that "in this church, we think change is a sin." He continued, "And we don't do much sinnin' around here."

In spite of the deacon's protest, all churches today are in transition and as we learned in the previous chapter, we need fresh understanding and new tools to do ministry well in these times. Change, like death and taxes, is inevitable. Interim ministry is the process of coming to terms with that change. Churches that navigate the change well during the interim time will reap positive benefits.

Most congregations require an interim minister after a pastor has tendered his or her resignation and is moving on. Ideally, it is a happy parting after a fruitful ministry together. The pastor has been well loved but parishioners feel his or her work is done and things seem to be running on autopilot. Likely, a serious review of the congregational character, purpose, calling, core values, and creative planning for the future has not happened in quite a while.

Still other pastors have left under a cloud due to conflict, controversy, or pastoral misconduct. The pastor may have been driven out by a small group of parishioners, which has split the congregation and created ill will all around.

Each of these situations would merit (and I would say require) an interim minister with skills to address the issues with which a congregation is struggling. The Interim Ministry Network (IMN) offers a training program to prepare intentional interim ministers for their role with a congregation.

The intentional interim minister receives specialized training to walk with congregations through the transitional time. There are three components to the IMN training, one focusing on the work of the leader and another on the work of the congregation. In addition, a field work project is required to apply the training. The training prepares the leader to address the needs of the congregation and to guide them as they work on their transition (or process) tasks. The leader enters the congregational system, analyzes the congregation, sets goals and focuses on specific tasks, connects with the community, evaluates and makes adjustments along the way, and then makes a healthy exit.

The next component of training is the work that a congregation does in response to the change event. Topics such as understanding the congregation's emotional system, discovering congregational norms and core values, addressing issues around differences or conflict, and finding strategies to best manage it are explored. An interim pastor also helps congregations discover their best practices and strengthens them and helps them find their purpose and mission. These are among many tools an interim minister will learn to use to guide the congregation through the time of transition.

Interim ministry is an art as well as a science, so taking an "off the rack" approach to every church will not work. An interim minister acts like a detective or archeologist, discovering congregational norms, folkways, and practices to lift out what is unique about the church. An interim ministry specialist follows a set of signposts called focus points. These focus points are not followed in a lockstep sequence but are adapted to each setting. These specific focus points were discerned through research and the experience of intentional interim ministers working with congregations in transition. The focus points are the work that a congregation does in response to the change event. They include heritage, leadership, mission, connections, and future, which I will discuss in greater detail in chapter 5.

In addition to specialized training, another factor in interim ministry is the time needed to work on the tasks of transition. The time limits are clearly specified in the contract the leader makes with the congregation before beginning the work. Depending upon the practices of a given denomination, the average pastoral search process takes between eighteen to twenty-four months. Usually two years is the maximum tenure, but the contract can be renegotiated to lengthen the agreement if necessary. Typically, an interim minister takes three months or so to enter the system of church life, getting to know the leaders, people, congregational style, and governance practices. During this time, the minister's goals are to develop a bird's eye view of the congregation and to understand the emotional system. He or she will then work with the leadership to set up a transitional team to work with and guide the pastor through the interim time. The team will select focus points and goals to work on during the time together and do assessments and readjustments along the way. [1]

FIVE THINGS CONGREGATIONS IN TRANSITION NEED TO KNOW

It's a no-brainer to say that all churches are in transition. With the landscape of American religion changing every time you blink your eyes, it's no wonder our congregations are reeling as they seek to make sense of and negotiate these new realities. It is my contention that all churches, whether established and settled with a twenty-year pastor or in transition because a pastor has left, are in flux.

In preparation for my book *Transitional Ministry Today: Successful Strategies for Churches and Pastors,* I spoke to dozens of practicing interim ministers, judicatory officials, and observers of American church life. Those conversations and my research became a collection of essays reflecting upon new models and practices in the face of the sea changes churches are facing. Here are some things I've learned. [2]

Interim Ministry Can Sometimes Be Scary and Unsettling

William Bridges did significant work in studying, developing theories, and helping organizations and businesses negotiate transitions. He came up with three simple, if not self-evident, "zones" through which people and organizations in transition travel. The first is the "letting go" stage where the work of mourning and saying goodbye is done. Next is the "neutral zone," which is really the transitional space between the past and the future, and the last is the "new beginning" zone. Bridges contends that it is not so much change that people resist or are uncomfortable with, but transition—the in-between time.[3] One of the most helpful ways to negotiate this time is to look at the past and recover practices, behaviors, norms, values, and attitudes that the congregation wants to bring forward into the future so it isn't so alien. To remember as individuals and as a church how you have negotiated change in the past and what coping skills worked well for you is a helpful practice during a time of change.

The diagram in figure 2.1 illustrates the three stages or zones of Bridges's theory. The horizontal axis, time, is the length of the transition. The vertical axis is how people react to the changes during the time of transition. Notice at the beginning on the left, almost everyone is having difficulty with the ending, while a few buy in almost immediately to a new beginning (white zone in top left). By the end of the transition, almost everyone has bought into the new beginning, while a few cannot let go of the ending.

In figure 2.2, we see the range of emotions people experience and behaviors people exhibit along the ups and downs of the interim time. People react or respond to changes differently according to their personalities or life experiences, just as they do grief. This is why transitions can be scary and unsettling.

There are ways the interim minister can help a congregation understand the dynamics of transition and change and how to manage them well. The practices are drawn from psychology, organizational development, and scripture.

In his groundbreaking *Generation to Generation: Family Process in Church and Synagogue*, Rabbi Edwin Friedman made the case that churches and synagogues are the institutions that operate most like a family emotional system.[4] Based upon the work of Murray Bowen, family systems theory is a theory of human behavior that views the family as an emotional unit and uses eight concepts that describe the complex interactions in the family unit. Just as nuclear families have social, physical, and organization interactions, they also have an emotional system they operate within. Emotional systems are patterns of behavior that happen within a network of relationships. Individual behavior is shaped

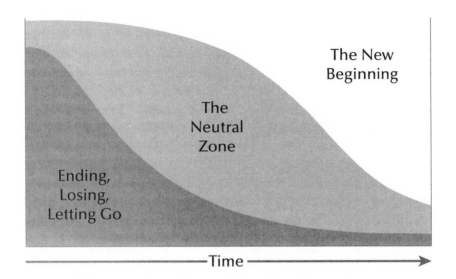

Managing Change: New Beginning Phase

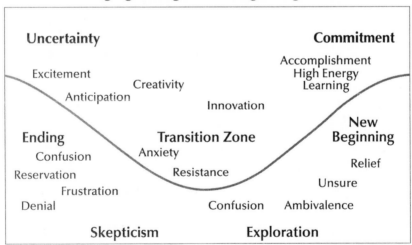

Figure 2.1. Adapted from *Managing Transitions*, **William Bridges.**

in reaction to the behavior of others. The goal of families or institutions is to keep things in "balance" or on an even keel emotionally. Changes and external forces introduced into the group disturb the balance, producing anxiety. Unfortunately, people manage the anxiety in unhelpful

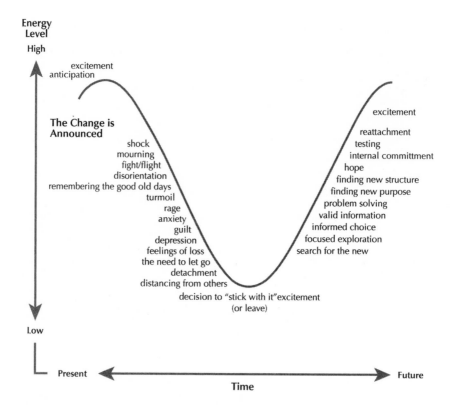

Figure 2.2.   From Gil Rendle, "The Roller Coaster of Change," *Alban Weekly,*
January 29, 2007.

or destructive ways. Often, the "issue" is not really the issue, but how people are processing the emotions.

Let me give you an example of how an emotional system works. In all families, parents and children play different roles. The parents may model a loving, equal partnership and in other families, mom or dad is clearly the leader. How families deal with differences, talk about and spend money, relate to their extended families, and manage family life are all learned behavior. All emotional systems like to maintain harmony or equilibrium, and when change is introduced, the system tries to restore balance.

Say that mom and dad are having difficulty in their marriage. They seem to be arguing more and spend more time apart. Suzy, who is usually well behaved and a great student, begins to act out and her grades drop. She becomes the identified "problem." Unconsciously, she is behaving badly so that the attention is focused on her and away from her parents' troubled marriage. The issue is not Suzy's bad behavior, but that mom and dad are having difficulties in their marriage.

Congregations manage change and difficult emotions in the same way. When anxiety rises in a church it unsettles the equilibrium that helps the congregation function. The introduction of a new hymnal, for instance, can unsettle a congregation. Parishioners have held the same hymnal in their hands on Sunday mornings for twenty-plus years. They like the old, familiar hymns that have sustained them over time.

The new hymnal has dropped some of their favorites, added world music and contemporary hymns, and changed the language so that it is inclusive of men, women, different races, and the physically challenged. Some people are distressed by the changes and feel that their preferences weren't respected. Instead of taking time to understand one another and the meanings they attach to hymns, people begin to accuse one another of not respecting tradition or being too stuck to change. In the end, when folks listened to one another they found that everyone wanted to sing at the top of their lungs during worship and some songs that inspire some congregants don't do a thing for others. This issue was not the hymnal per se, but the unidentified emotions underneath the decision to get a new hymnal. By identifying and talking through a range of feelings, the system righted itself.

With this brief introduction to emotional systems, we can understand that just by showing up, an interim minister will send ripples through the emotional workings of a church. Even if there was a healthy goodbye between the pastor and the people, a "new kid on the block" will be unfamiliar. Complicating the emotional system of a church even more is the grief at the departure of a beloved pastor or any accompanying anger or conflict about a pastor's departure, especially when clergy misconduct is involved.

Whenever change is introduced into an emotional system it creates anxiety or unease. People who are uncomfortable with anxiety often don't know how to manage it and like to pass it on as soon as they can, so they tell another person. This is called triangulation.

So if Jill is uncomfortable with the changes in worship or the selection of hymns the new minister has introduced, she will go to Mary to kvetch. Mary is uncomfortable with Jill's discomfort and wants to give *it* away, so she in turn tells someone else. Instead of going to the pastor or the music committee or the leadership, Jill went to Mary. What Mary should have done was reflect back the concern and encourage Jill to go directly to the pastor and thus break the triangle. She then wouldn't have to take on Jill's anxiety, and she wouldn't need to pass it on to yet another person.

The ability to separate your feelings and your thoughts is called self-differentiation. Self-differentiation refers to the degree to which a person can think and act for him or herself while dealing with an emotionally charged issue. A self-differentiated person is self-aware and does not absorb the emotions or positions of another, but defines herself.

Mary should have defined herself, saying something like, "Yes, it's hard to adjust to a new style of worship or music after having experienced another for many years, but I for one appreciate the changes. It will take some time to get used to, but as a church we need to make room for the variety of ways God speaks to people." Emotionally immature people find it difficult to manage their anxiety and self-differentiate so they tend to underfunction (not take responsibility for themselves and their jobs) or overfunction (do more than is required or expected of them). Pastors tend to do more of the later. Leaders in the church need to continue to hold those who underfunction accountable to do the work they promised to do. Congregations may also be tempted to rush the search process because it's uncomfortable and stressful instead of taking the time to take stock, do some self-reflection, and begin to plan for the future.

There is another way to understand congregational and family systems, but the focus is on the *structures* as opposed to the emotions of the system.[5] Paying attention to both is important. Systemic theory is based on the idea that parts (individuals) are inseparable from the whole (church, family, community, etc.). This theory is applied through what is called structural family therapy. Structural family therapy understands the congregation as a system that lives and operates within larger systems, such as a culture, the community, civil society, and the denomination. The congregational system, preferably, grows and changes over time. But sometimes a church gets stuck, often due to a dysfunction in the congregation's interactions or operations, called transactions.

Transactions are simply patterns of how church members routinely interact with each other. For example, a domineering board chair could be controlling and intimidating, overruling the decisions of a majority. There may be alliances, hierarchies, and routines that an interim minister can map to show the process that a congregation unconsciously follows. The goal, in the end, is to change the map or structure to help a church get "unstuck" from unhelpful transactions and structures that are aiding and abetting ongoing problems. An interim minister is not interested in figuring out how the problem pattern started, but is there to coach a church or board to find a different way of functioning. An interim minister can help churches strategically plan, execute, and measure "game winning" outcomes.[6]

Jay Haley, a key figure in applying structural family therapy, asserts that the emphasis of the intervention should not be on an individual but the positions or structures within the group.[7] There are often rules, dynamics, patterns, and rituals of behavior that an interim minister can help a church identify. Some of these norms are typical in congregations that are stuck:

- Only the clergy can do certain things like pastoral care or take communion to the homebound.
- Longevity, not certain competencies, gifts, and skills, is the only requirement needed to have more responsibility or leadership in the church.
- Chaos and conflict are bad things to be avoided, rather than signs of life to be embraced.
- Being nice is better than being truthful.
- People are not to be held accountable.
- A church should be run like corporate America.
- All we have to do is open the doors and people will come to our church.[8]

Take a few moments and think as an individual or as a group about some of the norms or ways your church is organized. Churches that are not self-aware of their norms and folkways can become "stuck" and not function effectively.

There are many biblical examples of times of transition, confusion, and how people reacted to them. Think of the Israelite nation wandering in the wilderness for forty years. This miracle worker Moses led them out of slavery and into new and unfamiliar territory. Following Moses was scary and the future was unknown. The Hebrew people were asking who is this man? He was in Pharaoh's court, wasn't he? Can we trust him? Where'd he get his authority? What if he was leading us out in the desert just to die? The Israelites had said goodbye to Egypt and there had been a dramatic ending. Now they were smack dab in the wilderness, the neutral zone. Some wanted to go back. Even though they were slaves in Egypt and lived under crushing circumstances, at least they knew the routine and had three squares a day and a place to sleep. Even though they had their eyes on the prize of the Promised Land, it was vague and hazy. The in-between time felt very uncomfortable. That is why they needed a visionary to lead them through the wilderness.

The movement from Good Friday through Holy Saturday to Easter Sunday is a New Testament example of a major shift or change. On Good Friday the disciples' dreams died. The man they had followed for these past three years was everything to them. They ate with him, slept with him, listened to him teach, watched him heal people and raise the dead. They saw him take on the religious and political establishment and hoped he was the Promised One. But now he was as dead as any dead man could be. Their dreams died with him. The horrible end of this fledgling Jesus movement was a colossal, overwhelming, and shocking end.

On Holy Saturday, they were lost in the wilderness. They couldn't wrap their heads around what had happened. They were in shock and disbelief and must have felt hopelessly abandoned. Even though Jesus had told them he would be killed and would rise again, they never really got it or believed it. It really wasn't just an in-between time because they had no idea what tomorrow would hold. They were in this horrible place.

But on Sunday morning, surprise! God raised the crucified Jesus from the dead and nothing would ever be the same again. Death, evil, and every privation of sin had been defeated. God indeed did have the last word! Where there had been despair there was now hope; where disappointment, now joy; disease, healing; cruelty, mercy; hatred, love. What had begun as something scary and unsettling finished with a new beginning in technicolor.

Interim Ministry Can Be Challenging and Exciting

As noted in the introduction, Loren Mead, Episcopal priest and church consultant, discovered that one of the most fertile times for church growth and vitality is between pastors. The first challenge is adjusting to new leadership and a new situation. Before a congregation calls a new pastor, they need time to let the field lie fallow for a while, so to speak. One of the purposes of the interim time is to have the congregation experience ministry under different pastoral leadership before calling a new pastor.

The importance of having a time of adjustment is well illustrated by an example familiar to us all. The Monks of the New Skete is an order in upstate New York that raises German shepherds as its calling and ministry. In their wonderful book, *How to Be Your Dog's Best Friend: A Training Manual for Dog Owners*, they advise that after a dog has died you should wait at least a month before you get another one. Not only do you need to grieve the loss of your companion animal, but you should let your home "air out." You need to take time to let the odors and the presence of your dog dissipate. Putting away the toys, bed, bowl, or special blanket that belonged to your previous pet is necessary before inviting a new dog into your home.[9]

Not to draw the comparison too tightly, but in the same way, a congregation shouldn't rush to fill a pastoral vacancy. Take time to reflect and to enjoy the process. The previous minister's fingerprints are everywhere in the church (literally and metaphorically), so churches need to take some time to learn to be a congregation without his or her presence.

It is also a time to do some essential self-study, which may not have been possible previously. An interim minister holds up a mirror to the congregation so they can see themselves more clearly. There are three important questions that a congregation must answer during the in-between time:

- Who are we? (questions of identity, core values, bedrock beliefs, norms)
- Who is our neighbor? (questions of demographics, the hopes and hurts of the community, and an alignment of those with the gifts and graces of the congregation)

- What is God calling us to do and to be? (questions of purpose, mission, vision, and planning)

We will be looking more closely at these three questions in the next chapter.

During a transitional period, a congregation can experience a different style of clergy leadership, variety in worship, and different programming if appropriate. These can be experiments that the congregation' tries, reflects upon, and decides to keep, tweak, or discard. A vital congregation may already be doing great things in these areas and a wise interim will keep her mitts off.

The early church operated in an experimental and adaptive manner in their beginning. In the Book of Acts, leaders in the church appeared to be making practices up as they went along. Each new situation they encountered presented a new challenge. Gentiles received the Holy Spirit, so what do we do about them? Some Christians were eating meat sacrificed at pagan temples. Some had guilty consciences about it and others didn't. What should the local leaders do? The wealthy were showing up at community gatherings early, eating and drinking; when the working poor or slaves arrived there was nothing left to eat and some of the earlier worshipers were drunk. How do we handle that? Each generation of the church has new sets of challenges that they need to face creatively, lovingly, and wisely. This can be the exciting work of the interim time.

Interim Ministry Is More Important Than You Think

Without doing the work of self-reflection and vision casting, a church will not be prepared to call a new pastor to lead them into the next chapter of their life together. When a congregation works together to discern their core values, purpose and mission, patterns of behavior, and the future to which God is calling them, it can be an exciting and inspiring process that binds people together. By making a hurried or unreflective decision to call a new pastor, the church might go back to business as usual or have a short-term pastor because of differing expectations or poor preparation. Calling a new pastor without doing this important work would be much like starting to date immediately after a divorce. Beware of the rebound or moving too quickly.

An interim pastor is a detective gathering clues and data that helps a congregation see how it functions. She is also an archeologist, digging up treasures that may have been hidden for good or for ill. The interim minister looks over the congregation from the balcony, viewing the congregation as an emotional system, observing how a congregation deals with stress, noting its best practices and norms, how they deal with differences, and what they should celebrate about themselves. The interim has one foot in the congregation as shepherd and pastor and one foot out as an observer of congregational life.

Important work can and should be done during the interim time. Significant ministry need not stop. While it's time to take stock and reflect, it is not necessary to lose momentum. Pilot projects can be tested, new worship styles can be experimented with, different small groups can be offered, and more efficient governance structures can be looked at as examples.

In the book of Genesis we see the Holy Spirit hovering over the waters of creation bringing order out of chaos. This activity was as if God was experimenting and was delightfully surprised when something new popped up, like a duck or a strawberry. Churches too can look for the Spirit guiding and leading in creative ways during a time of transition. At times the Spirit's movement may seem odd or unfamiliar, but some fun and unexpected things can pop up as well. By faith, we know that the Spirit is active in the midst of transition, bringing order and beauty out of the seeming chaos.

The mystic Francis Fenelon said, "The Spirit is always blowing, but we must hoist a sail." In other words, something is always happening; the Spirit is blowing. It's a time to do the important work of learning to listen for the Spirit. Look for what the Spirit's doing and get on board!

The Interim Time May Last Longer Than You Think (Or It Might Not)

Pastoral searches vary in length depending upon denominational polity, the length of the previous pastorate, and the amount of work required on the focus points. While most pastoral searches take between eighteen and twenty-four months, there may be delays because scheduling search committee interviews with candidates can be difficult, a crisis may emerge, or perhaps a conflict that was buried pops up and must be dealt with. A candidate may decline an offer or take another call. Neither does a search committee want to drag its feet and lose momentum. Remember that the Spirit blows where it will and the timetable of God may be different from that of the search committee or the candidates.

Further, there are issues that might emerge that need to be addressed before a new pastor arrives. Perhaps a staff member or two leaves or someone is fired, necessitating a search and replacement before a new pastor can be called. A congregation may wish to use the time to come up with a new governance model or rewrite the by-laws before a new pastor arrives, or there may be some unresolved conflict or issue or prior unethical behavior that needs to be addressed before a new pastor is on the scene.

A bridge interim is a pastor who serves a church as a bridge between a lengthy interim period and the call of a settled pastor. I served a church as a bridge interim after they had had an interim minister for twenty-seven months. They were discouraged because they hadn't pulled the trigger and called a pastor they liked soon enough and she took another position. Others turned them down because they thought the congregation wasn't a good fit or they wanted to live in a community with better school systems. They became very dispirited until one day a resume came from a pastor who had experience turning urban churches around. If they had settled and just hired someone to get it over with, they would have missed out on the person God had for them. Remember to be mindful of God's providential, behind-the-scenes activity during the search process.

The Interim Process Should Be Embraced (But Honor How Each Person Negotiates Change)

People tolerate pain or discomfort differently. Those who don't tolerate it well want to move quickly to get back to their previous comfort level. Some of you may be familiar with the Myers-Briggs Type Indicator, which measures personality preferences. The polarities are Introverted or Extroverted (finding restoration by being alone or with others), Sensing (using the five senses to make decisions) or Intuition (going with your gut), Thinking (using logic and consistency when evaluating a situation) or Feeling (taking people and relationships into consideration when making decisions), and Judging (making orderly and structured decisions whether using the Thinking or Feeling function) or Perceiving (being more flexible and open-ended in decision making). None of these categories is meant to pigeonhole anyone. Our preferences are more of our default positions.

Those, for instance, who are Js in the Myer-Briggs scheme like things done decently and in order and find their anxiety reduced once a decision has been made. Those who are Ps generally like to gather more information and might find their anxiety heightened somewhat once a decision is made. Introverts or Extroverts might be attracted to a candidate who is closer to their personality type. An extrovert may be very open and direct with an opinion about a candidate and think out loud. Introverts may be quiet, ask thoughtful questions, and need time to process their decisions.

Leaders in the church, a transition team, or the search committee each need to be aware of these emotional and interpersonal dynamics. Together you can better understand how some members who seem to be resisting the transitional tasks could simply need time to take it all in before making decisions. Others may want to collect a lot of data before making decisions, and others are more concerned about making sure everyone is heard and relationships remain strong. We need to honor the unique way God has made each one when it comes to collecting information, evaluating it, and making decisions.

Often the best work happens when people are in conversation about things that are most important to them. Using the in-between time to help people build emotional and spiritual bonds, lift up the values they share, and honor the experiences that create meaning are often more important than writing the perfect profile or finding the textbook pastor.

In summary, transitional ministry is the work of a congregation and an intentional interim minister together to bring the people of God from the end of one era of ministry (through the wilderness of discerning together and trusting God to bring them to a new future) and embracing that future with full and open hearts. Some of God's best work is done during times of transition. Think of the Israelites learning their true identity as God's covenant people while in the desert. Or think of Jesus getting clarity about his call while spending forty days in the Judean wilderness. On our journey toward the resurrection, during transition times, we discover our true selves. For many, it is a fearful experience of testing, but one that is moderated by a special grace: we make this journey together, with your local congregation, with the whole Christian church on earth, and we follow the One who has already completed the course.

QUESTIONS FOR REFLECTION AND DISCUSSION

1. What is your understanding after having read this chapter of the importance of having an intentional interim or transitional minister?
2. What do you think of Bridges's model of transition? Where do you see evidence of it in your church?
3. What are some of the reasons your church could benefit from an interim pastor?

EXERCISE

The roller coaster of change shows a natural progression of feelings we experience in a time of transition. It also may indicate how far along we are in accepting and owning the change. (Refer back to figure 2.2.) As a group, take a few minutes to explore your own feelings during a time of change.

- Recall a time of great change in your life. It does not matter whether the change was positive and exciting (the birth of a child) or negative and difficult (a divorce or the loss of a job).
- Begin at the point where you first received news of this change and begin to recall the feelings you experienced as you lived through the change.
- Pay attention to the sequence in which you recall or experience the feelings, list them on a sheet of newsprint.
- Compare your list of feelings to the roller coaster of change chart. How were your feelings the same as or different from the ones on the chart? Did they follow the same sequence?

3

WHY DO WE NEED AN INTERIM MINISTER?

There was a time when interim ministers were not seen as a necessity. Establishment churches were very much a part of American culture, as we saw in the section on American civil religion. Everyone knew what needed to be done—get someone in to deliver religious goods and services. Things like leading worship, preaching, visiting the sick, baptisms, weddings, funerals, and teaching confirmation. The pastor was more of a chaplain than a leader.

In the same way, we wouldn't want a student who just graduated from medical school doing brain surgery on us. However, we shouldn't want a minister who has not received any special training or had any experience in transitional ministry leading us in an interim time. This is not to discount the effectiveness of any clergyperson, but to underscore the need for expertise in the field. We don't need a criminal lawyer when drawing up a last will and testament, but we do for criminal activity.

As we saw in chapter 1, the culture has changed, the church has changed, and the mission has changed. Churches don't know what to do. Christendom has passed. Church attendance isn't an expectation. Christianity is one of many choices in the marketplace of ideas. How are we to navigate these choppy waters?

One of the first jobs of a transitional minister is to bring stability and calm during a time of transition. The announcement that the pastor is leaving, under any circumstances, sends a jolt through the emotional system of a church. Oftentimes, what a church needs, particularly after a church has had a difficult ending with its pastor, is someone who will show up and do a steady job of preaching, leading worship, and offering pastoral care.

When a long-term pastor leaves a congregation, the norms and expectations set up by the long tenure may be difficult for the pastor that follows. An intentional interim minister allows a congregation to experience different approaches to ministry and opens eyes to different styles of pastoral leadership. The role of the interim minister is not to shake things up per se but to become part of the congregation, paying attention to the values, norms, practices, and ethos of the congregation. An interim minister plays many roles, including shepherd, preacher, spiritual guide, worship leader, counselor, and more. But there are some unique roles that interim ministers play.

A transitional minister also helps a church to set a fresh course. When a church feels it's at a difficult crossroad, quick decisions may be made by the leadership or at a congregational meeting without fully exploring options and potential outcomes. An interim minister can slow down the call process, allowing the congregation time to make well-informed and deliberate decisions regarding the future course of the church. Using tools and theories such as church life cycles, along with the dynamics of church size, cottage meetings, small groups, and all church events, fertile discussions will take place to tease out themes, values, and visions of the community.

A time of transition presents a wonderful opportunity for a church to take stock of where they are as a congregation and enter into a time of self-discovery. This is an appropriate time to reflect upon important questions, such as What is our purpose? Do we have a clear mission and vision? Where are our strengths, weaknesses, opportunities, and threats? Where is health we can nurture? Does our structure and stewardship best support the work we are to do? Asking these questions will enable a church to make well-informed, thoughtful decisions about the next chapter of their life together.

Gil Rendle and Alice Mann in their book *Holy Conversations: Strategic Planning as a Spiritual Practice* assert that the three essential questions a congregation needs to answer during a time of transition are "Who are we?" "Who is our neighbor?" and "What is God calling us to do and become?"[1]

• **Who are we?** This question addresses the issue of identity. Each church has an identity whether conscious or not. They may be the church that houses the food pantry or the church that has the pie festival at Christmastime or an amazing music program. Almost every church I know describes themselves as "friendly," which is often the perception they have of themselves, not necessarily shared by outsiders. Another one is "this church is like family."

Identity goes deeper than this. Identity is that consistent set of norms, rituals, core values, and bedrock beliefs that make a congregation distinctively itself. Program is the "face" with which congregations present themselves, but identity is the self-image congregations carry, even when it is unknown or unstated. Identity is what makes your church unique and distinguishes it from other congregations. It includes things like norms—how decisions are made, the role of the pastor, the place of children in church, and how the church manages conflict. It is about history. Who are the saints, heroes, and villains in the church's memory? When were you at your best or your worst? It is about rituals. How is communion served? How does your church conduct rites of passage such as baptism, confirmation, marriage, and death? How is the annual meeting run?

Core values are another important piece of identity. What nonnegotiable values drive programs and activities? Are high-quality worship and music a priority? What kind of behavior is acceptable or unacceptable? Is Christian education and formation a priority for your congregation when planning programs?

Bedrock beliefs should be identified. This is not the statement of faith or doctrine that is adhered to or required for membership (though they could be), but more like rock-bottom convictions: God answers prayer, telling and doing the Good News are important, God and God's people have carried me through hard times, and if anyone has a need we will not turn them away because Jesus didn't. [2]

Stories make up the warp and woof of every congregation. They carry the collective memories, history, and ideals of its members. They include tales about the chicken potpie supper the vestry ran for years, the time the pastor's son lowered the chandelier in the sanctuary during worship, or Mrs. Magilicutty who taught Sunday school since the earth cooled. The stories congregations tell says a lot about their soul.

• **Who is our neighbor?** Asking this question helps your congregation discover the hurts and hopes of your surrounding community. Every congregation lives within and is shaped by its environment. Included
in the social context are characteristics of a neighborhood: Is it residen-
tial or commercial? Where do people hang out? Is it tree lined or
lacking green space? What do people do for a living? And is it an old
neighborhood or new? Social context also includes the racial and ethnic
mix of people, civic and social groups, and the various political and
economic forces at work in the setting. This is the framework within
which the church does its ministry. An interim minister can help a
congregation understand its social realities, which is immensely helpful
when shaping their mission and in designing ministries.

Congregations often think they know their neighborhood or community without ever having tested those assumptions. Answering this question may well help parishioners see how much their neighborhood or
city has changed, which new populations are moving in, and what needs
they were not aware of.

The best place to begin answering this question is by gathering demographic and census data. Two excellent resources for demographic
data for churches are MissionInsite (http://missioninsite.com/) and Percept (http://www.perceptgroup.com/). In addition to providing information about population size, educational and income levels, and so on,
MissionInsite measures worship preferences, use of social media, lifestyle choices, and ministries people might look for. Interviews with
community leaders, neighborhood walks, and random sample surveys
with neighbors are other ways to collect data to help discern "who is my
neighbor."

• **What is God calling us to be and to do?** Struggling with this
question assists a congregation in discovering its purpose, vision, and
mission. The answers that come from answering "Who are we?" and
"Who is our neighbor?" provide the foundation for answering this question. Through a period of reflection and prayer, a congregation can
determine the defining direction of the church, the reason for its being,
and their "elevator speech"—the answer you would give if someone you
met in an elevator asked, "What is your church all about?" You've got
thirty seconds to reply. The elevator speech answers the question, "If
St. Johns by the 7-Eleven closed, what would be missing from this
town?"

Note that this question includes what God is calling the congregation to *be* and to *do*. Churches know how to do things, especially how to keep the organization functioning, as well as how to conduct mission trips, serve at soup kitchens, or bring communion to homebound folks. They are less adept at learning how "to be" as a people before God and for one another. This "being" question looks at the character and spirit of a church and asks questions like

- How do we behave together?
- What feeds our souls spiritually so we are equipped to do our "activities"?
- How are we helping people to discover their spiritual gifts in service of ministry?
- What are ways we show respect and appreciation for one another?
- Are children an important part of our congregation? If so, how do we show it?

"What is God calling us to do?" is the second part of the mission question. The mission is the particular and peculiar task(s) that God has for a congregation to advance the Gospel in their time and place and with the gifts of its members. It should be conceived by letting the answers to "Who are we?" and "Who is our neighbor?" gestate for a while and give birth to a "preferred future," or to a vision of tomorrow. It should be a bold statement that requires faith and imagination to achieve.

By answering these three questions, a church will discover its missional identity, which will inform strategic planning and goal setting. An interim minister has a set of skills, practices, and exercises to help congregations wrestle with these questions in fun and enlightening ways.

In addition to helping congregational leaders answer three questions, interim ministers help churches achieve three tasks. My colleague Don Remick says that transitional ministers are to help congregations become healthy, faithful, and effective.[3]

"Healthy" refers to how a congregation processes information, deals with disagreements, communicates with one another, and balances outreach with inreach. An effective interim minister can help healthy churches become healthier and unhealthy churches become healthy.

"Faithful" refers to the primary reason for the existence of a congregation. Are we seeking God's face and direction in all that we do? Do we bathe everything in prayer? Are we looking to scripture to inform our values and decision making?

"Effective" means we are getting the job done. It makes no difference if we're healthy and faithful if we're not making a difference. Are lives being touched and changed? Are we growing in faith? Are people being fed or clothed or visited? Are our children being well prepared to be Christians in the world? Do we stand up to injustice? Let's look at each of these tasks more closely.

There are scores of different models of what constitutes a faithful, healthy, and effective church. I am aware of at least fourteen. For the most part they agree that vital churches have Spirit-filled worship, significant relational groups that provide opportunities for care giving and making disciples, outreach programs of both benevolence and justice, and streamlined governance structures. I find Remick's presentation to be a succinct and helpful summary. Let me elaborate on the three marks of dynamic churches.

What are the characteristics of a healthy church?

- Healthy churches are where people feel safe to be themselves without rejection, criticism, or pressure to conform. People are free to share their thoughts, values, and ideas and welcome those from others as well. Differences are welcomed as a normal part of the human family. The congregation, and its leaders in particular, set boundaries around unacceptable and inappropriate behavior. Bullying is not tolerated and no one may shame, blame, or attack another.

- Healthy churches are transparent. Boards and committees are open to all and minutes are accessible. Finances are clear, transparent, and accessible to anyone. Decision- and policymaking processes are clear and members are able to learn how decisions are made, who made them, and the rationale behind them. Members don't have secret meetings in the parking lot, at a coffee shop, or in their homes, but keep their concerns in the open.

- Healthy churches have direct communication. If members have a problem or concern, they go directly to the person involved, including the pastor(s). They speak for themselves and not for others. They also understand that having your say doesn't necessarily mean having your way.

- Healthy churches aren't afraid of conflict. Conflict means a body of people is alive and well. People respond to anxiety and change instead of reacting to it. A healthy church will have venues to share conflicts and policies and procedures everyone follows. Conflict is not bad, but dealing with conflict by trying to get others in your corner, painting those who disagree with you as "bad guys," or pretending it isn't there is unhealthy. Large people talk about ideas; small people talk about others.

- Healthy churches are places where forgiveness is freely given and received. We all are one at the foot of the cross—sinners in need of God's grace and redemption. We shouldn't be surprised when we sin or someone sins against us, but we should be able to model how a community of faith struggles to keep its accounts short and play fair.

- Healthy churches recognize that in God's wisdom we are an emotional system. Just as our bodies comprise many different but interdependent systems, so do our churches. We try to keep emotional stability and when tension is introduced into the system (the pastor makes changes in the worship service or the deacons make a decision not everyone agrees with) the system then pushes back to try to find equilibrium. Sometimes we just have to live with the tension for a while and see where the Spirit leads us.

- Healthy congregations focus on their strengths rather than their weaknesses. They are not "problem saturated." They don't try to be something they're not.

- Healthy congregations make stewardship an ongoing process. Members understand that supporting the church is not just "paying their fair share," but an important piece of their spiritual growth. Generous and enthusiastic giving describes their attitude toward giving. Plans are in place for a sustainable future.

- Healthy churches focus on mission, rather than on getting along, the past, survival, the minister, or some other concern. The mission of loving God, sharing Christ, and ministering to people drives every decision.

- Healthy congregations act flexibly and creatively, adapting to new challenges instead of rigidly relying on precedent, Robert's Rules, or bylaws, realizing that every problem does not have a quick fix. New truths require new practices and that takes discernment.

- Healthy churches practice hospitality by welcoming the stranger, the newcomer, and the outsider instead of showing favoritism for the few or likeminded. People empower others rather than dominate or cure them. People develop caring relationships and share their lives instead of each living for oneself.

What are the characteristics of a faithful church?

- A faithful church offers worship services that are challenging, inspiring, and joyful regardless of whether they are traditional, contemporary, blended, or contemplative. Laughter and silence are both regular features. A faithful church provides regular encounters with the living God. People come to worship not to hear a religious lecture or to hear fine music but to experience the Holy and the Transcendent One.
- A faithful church makes decisions by thoughtful prayer and discernment, not by a simple majority or by following Robert's Rules of Order. God speaks most clearly through people who are gathered together in covenant.
- A faithful church as a whole participates in caring and advocacy for "the least of these." These responsibilities are not simply delegated to a mission or the "Called to Care" ministry. Service is taught and understood as a part of spiritual growth.
- A faithful church sees making disciples as more of a priority than just adding members. Members are moving from being volunteers to becoming intentional disciples by participating in programs that teach and practice spiritual formation. Faithful churches provide plenty of access points to participate in congregational life for those who are not interested in institutional membership.
- A faithful church assumes responsibility to pass along the faith to children and adults. Parents are trained to provide spiritual formation for their families. Christian formation is not simply relegated to the Christian Education director or the pastor who provides adult education opportunities and leads confirmation.

- A faithful church is one where all members of the congregation engage in spiritual practices and faith formation. This could be in a small group such as a Bible study, prayer circle, or at home churches, as well as through service and mission projects. Churches provide opportunity for people to discover and apply their spiritual gifts as they live out their call or vocation.
- A faithful church is willing to take risks, fail, and learn from the experience. This could be with programming within the church or outreach into the community. Congregations will work from an "action/reflection" mode where they experiment and reflect upon what worked and what didn't, what to keep and what to discard.
- A faithful church will find that as people grow in faith and faithfulness, stewardship of time, talent, and treasure will increase.

What are the characteristics of an effective church?

- An effective church is making an impact in its community and world. It will have a reputation in the community as a church that makes a difference in the character and quality of members' lives and in their city or town.
- An effective church knows the surrounding community and the changes in the religious landscape. Members are exploring the demographics, values, and faith styles of the community along with history, trends, and projections. They have conversations with community leaders to keep abreast of human needs.
- An effective church is seeing its worship attendance increase. Regular members are coming with more frequency and the number of visitors is increasing.
- An effective church is one that participates in the community to build relationships and networks. This could be with government officials, social service agencies, local schools, civic organizations, sports activities, and cultural groups.
- An effective congregation is actively and purposely listening to those who have a spiritual hunger but do not believe in institutional religion or find it particularly meaningful. They often refer to themselves as "spiritual, but not religious." The goal is to understand and appreciate seekers without necessarily trying to get them to come to church.

- An effective congregation has a system in place to heartily welcome visitors, record their attendance, and follow up with them,
not just those who attended worship but anyone who attended
other programs at the church.
- An effective church will find members and regular participants
describing their lives as being transformed by their involvement in
and relationship with the congregation.

These are high and lofty standards and take hard work and perseverance to implement them. Do these descriptors of a church sound like a
congregation you'd like to be part of? How does your church measure
up? Where might you begin?

BUGS IN THE SYSTEM

During the transitional time an interim leader can help congregations,
particularly leaders, deal with negative patterns of behavior and difficult
issues that perennially pop up. Congregations, like families, don't allow
us to pick who's in and who's out. In church we often rub shoulders
with people with whom we might not ordinarily mix. They might be of
another generation with different tastes, preferences, and understandings about life and church. This can be a source of great joy and great
annoyance. But how else will we learn to love those who are totally
unlike us, be patient with those who drive us nuts, or be blessed with
gifts from others that come as a surprise?

An interim minister can help you identify "viruses" that may be
present in the emotional system of your church. There are behaviors in
any church that are not healthy and can become contagious. Boundaries
might be crossed with unacceptable conduct. Viruses need a host. They
do not survive independently but need a body to live in. The church can
be a body where viruses live, but they need to be quarantined.

At one church where I did a workshop on healthy leadership, the
presenting issue was a subcommittee of the trustees that chose to replace the traditional red velvet carpet in fellowship hall with a more
modern mauve. Those who objected did an end run around the committee and started a campaign to undo their decision.

Another unhealthy practice might be letting those with the loudest voices dominate public meetings or allowing bullying behavior without calling out the offender. Perhaps not having open, transparent, and clear lines of communication leaves some feeling that there is an in-group who wields all the decision-making power. Whatever the virus is, it is best to isolate and inoculate it so it can't spread.

Gil Rendle, a United Methodist minister and seasoned author and church consultant, argues that a behavioral covenant is an essential document to craft for any congregation.[4] A behavioral covenant promotes wholesome, transparent, and respectful communication, especially during times of disagreement. Such a covenant puts in writing how people want "to be" in their congregational life together. It is especially useful to do this during an interim time. After looking at scriptural expectations for household behavior in the Body of Christ, participants brainstorm behaviors to help them live in the covenant. They are practices such as

- Treat one another with respect.
- Only speak for yourself and not for others.
- Use "I" statements.
- Listen to understand before presenting a counterargument.
- Agree to disagree and act agreeably, and so on.

After the covenant is drafted, the congregation should study and ratify it to get everyone's buy-in. The leadership of the congregation should model the covenant with one another. With such guidelines, both the leadership and the church can hold one another accountable. More important, rather than being a tool to "keep people in line," members can grow in grace and learn skills that will build health into a congregation. An example of a behavioral covenant is found in appendix A.

Setting appropriate boundaries with a behavioral covenant or a policy manual promotes healthy communication and conduct. Boundaries limit access to relationships, information, and decision making. They might include: Are relationships among members honored with honesty and integrity, without keeping secrets or sabotaging each other's work or personhood? Is confidential information that is shared repeated indiscriminately among other members of the congregation? When boards and committees make decisions appropriate to its authority and according to the rules and roles of the system, do church members abide by those decisions? Do people respect the office of the pastor? Do people honor the pastor's days off and family time?

Having a clear mission and vision statement to return to is always important when some individuals try to get the church off track of its purpose. If the congregation ratified it, leaders can say, "As a church we decided that more of our pastor's time should be spent in the community and not just with our parishioners. This was part of our mission to reach out to the community." The mission should always chart the course.

Knowing and reminding the congregation of their core values is equally important, perhaps more so than crafting a mission statement. An interim minister will lead the congregation through a process to discover and affirm those. An example of core values is found in appendix B. These values are a significant subtext of your congregation's story and knowing them can help keep you on track with your purpose and mission. Core values indicate what is important to your people, what shapes your community, and what drives mission. Core values should be congruent with the character of the congregation and serve to remind people this is what their church is about. They are the moral dimension of a community: its values, preferred behavioral tone, character, and communal norms. Through these values the congregation sees and interprets the word; character defines the group's preferences and values. A worldview reveals what a congregation thinks is going on; character tells what they wish would go on.

When leaders remind congregants of their values and mission then it is more difficult for members to focus critically on what the pastor is doing (or not doing), how we spend our money, or what Bibles we give to confirmands. Too often churches say they want programs they think they should want.

A word of caution, however, when dealing with bugs in the system, whether it's disruptive behavior or boundary crossing. When we say there may be "unhealthy" behavior going on in a church, we must be careful not to pathologize a congregation by giving the impression that the whole body is sick. In some cases that may be true, but in most cases, it is likely a bacteria or virus that needs to be isolated or eliminated from the system. If we use a medical model alone to diagnose church dynamics, then the church can become the presenting patient, the pastor or leaders the attending physician, and the cure not always useful.

My colleague Rob Voyle often offers this advice in these situations: it is better to use the word "unhelpful" when describing or confronting someone about disruptive behaviors. People are less defensive than if you call them or their behavior "unhealthy." It may become unhealthy if it escalates. The behavior is unhelpful if it violates the behavioral covenant, hurts people, knocks the church off the track of its mission, keeps boards and committees from doing their work, or brings a pall over the spirit of the congregation.

Remember, however, that positive emotions are also contagious! Just as negativity can be infectious, so can positivity. Edwin Friedman, the rabbi and psychologist who wrote the classic book *Generation to Generation,* said that anxiety is the most contagious emotion in families, churches, and synagogues.[5] It's much like coming home from school or work with a nasty cold and sneezing on everyone—they catch the cold too. I think we all have experienced how negativity, sarcasm, cynicism, anger, criticism, and bad moods can infect a whole household or community—that's the bad news. The good news is that our positive moods—joy, peace, humor, love, and happiness—are also contagious. We can just as easily "infect" people around us with our positive energy as we can with our negative energy.

What we focus on becomes our reality. That is why promoting health is so much more important than combatting disease. In Galatians 5, Paul lays out a list of vices and virtues. First, he lists things like enmities, strife, jealousy, anger, quarrels, dissensions, factions, drunkenness, and carousing (Galatians 5: 19–21). But Paul never simply lists things to avoid without next listing things to which Christians should aspire. He calls them the "fruit of the Spirit." Things like love, joy, peace, patience, kindness, generosity, faithfulness, gentleness, and self-control (5: 22–23).

SPECIAL CIRCUMSTANCES

Situations present themselves that particularly require an experienced intentional interim minster. A time of healing may be needed, especially after clergy misconduct, a significant congregational conflict, or a natural disaster. Without healing existing divisions within the church, it is difficult to have a unified mission and ministry. Further, a congregation may have to learn communication skills, anger management, and mature leadership skills of being able to listen, be objective, show compassion, and act in the interest of the whole congregation. There are also circumstances where congregations feel manipulated or misled by their former pastor and need guidance to become whole again. They need assistance in developing an attitude of trust toward pastoral leadership. These are situations that simply take time to untangle. It is important to do what is necessary to reach understanding and closure through a safe and caring process that leads to a thorough resolution.

An interim minister may also be asked to lead a congregation through a particular task. I served a church once when all of the leadership and many in the congregation had read Anthony Robinson's book *Transforming Congregational Culture*.[6] In so doing, they were already familiar with the dynamics of changing culture and shifts in how "to do church" in the twenty-first century. They were eager to put into practice what they had learned. I was tasked to help them discover a purpose statement, mission, and vision. We were able to do so with broad congregational participation, which generated positive energy.

At two other settings the leadership wanted to explore a new organizational structure that was "lean and mean" and that recognized new models of organization, ways changing lifestyles of leaders in their church impacted their time and energy, and opportunities to streamline policies and procedures. In both cases they restructured, rewriting the bylaws to be more flexible and missional and creating teams instead of boards or committees. The teams were able to do a lot of their work online or by telephone and met as needed.

Lastly, the interim pastor can be a tremendous help to various boards and committees. Boards may need help bringing closure to the former pastor's ministry; dealing with difficult people; resolving issues of leadership, ministries, or structure; strengthening the Christian education program; or addressing other issues left from the previous pastor's tenure. An evaluation of the church's ministries, a review of job descriptions and personnel policies, as well as the functions of each board or committee might be in order during this transition period. During the interim, the church's leaders and members may be under more stress than usual and can lose focus on their mission. An interim pastor can help keep them on track.

While the relationship an interim has with the search committee needs to be circumspect, he or she can still be helpful to this group. An interim minister might coach the search committee in their tasks and review the parish profile to see if it accurately reflects who the congregation is. Interim ministers do not get involved at all with the search process beyond that. The committee may not ask them about specific candidates they are considering. They must, however, keep the interim appraised of their progress with a search so he or she is aware if the search committee is approaching a call with a candidate.

This is a thumbnail sketch of why churches need an intentional interim ministry during a transitional period. Churches can negotiate with an interim minister about the kinds of issues, projects, and problems they want to address during their time together. Interim ministry is not a cookie-cutter or one-size-fits-all methodology. Recognizing that each church has its unique personality, an interim minister will work with leadership to tailor a mutual ministry to accomplish a set of agreed-upon goals. With the help of an interim pastor, however, the church can emerge from the time between settled pastors stronger and with a renewed vision for its purpose and mission. This strength in turn helps the new pastor as he or she assumes leadership.

QUESTIONS FOR REFLECTION AND DISCUSSION

1. Of the above reasons given for having an intentional interim pastor, which one(s) best fit your congregation?
2. How would you answer the three questions: Who are we? Who is our neighbor? and What is God calling us to do and to be?
3. How would your church measure up against the criteria of healthy, faithful, and effective? As a group, go through the questions in appendix C, "Gut Check: Twenty-Five Key Questions to Measure Church Vitality," and see what you learn.

4

WHO SHOULD WE HIRE?

There's a story online about an applicant who showed up late for an interview wearing a long trench coat with his hair slicked back in a ponytail. As the interview progressed, he answered the recruiting manager's questions, sipped on his Starbucks coffee, and tilted the chair on the back legs. When asked the question, "Why should I hire you?" he responded by taking a sip, leaning way back, running his hand along the side of his hair, and saying, "Because I'm so good looking."

Hiring an interim or settled minister should not be a beauty contest. Think about it. Often the search committee spends only a few hours with the candidate. He or she comes for the weekend to schmooze, lead worship and preach, maybe teach a class. Then the congregation votes and calls the pastor. You have just thrown your lot in together in a pretty intimate way based upon a very short relationship.

God's advice to Samuel when searching for a king for Israel is apt here. "God sees not as humanity sees, for humanity looks at the outward appearance, but the Lord looks at the heart" (1 Samuel 16: 7). Remember, Jesse showed Samuel all his strapping sons, but Samuel wasn't satisfied and asked if there were anymore. "Yes," said Jesse, "but he's the runt of the litter and is out tending sheep." That runt was David. You know the rest of the story. Too often our churches call a pastor who is gregarious, engaging, and well put together. He wowed them during the interview process and preached a stellar sermon. But the Search Committee discovered in a short while that they really needed someone to lead them into their future and help them achieve their vision. Even though the new pastor was quite competent, he didn't have the skills to lead them to their next step.

Hiring an effective transitional minister is almost as important as hiring an effective long-term pastor. The work you do together will significantly till the soil so that noteworthy success and vitality can be achieved after your new pastor arrives. You want to make sure that your interim pastor is fully qualified, well trained, and experienced—not like our Starbucks-drinking candidate above.

Sometimes churches think that hiring a part-time pulpit supply or a retired minister on the cheap after a settled pastor has left is a good way to save money. While you may save money, other costs can be much greater. You might rob yourself of doing the important work of assessment and self-study. You could lose the opportunity to look carefully at issues that may have been buried or unresolved. You may miss a chance to be exposed to another style of ministry and experiment with creative ideas for mission, worship, and Christian education.

A quality interim pastor will move you through the five focus points discussed in chapter 2—heritage, leadership, mission, connections, and future—as appropriate for your congregation. This person will be your spiritual guide, teacher, caregiver, comforter, challenger, and friend for years to come. This is someone you will grow to love, trust, and look to for leadership. It is not a choice that should be made easily or too quickly. Remember, hiring a pastor is not like hiring an administrative assistant.

Paul Nickerson of Nickerson Coaching has developed an assessment tool for evaluating pastoral candidates.[1] His first step in hiring, whether an interim or a settled pastor, is a prayer and discernment process asking for the guidance of the Holy Spirit. It is critical for a search committee not only to bathe themselves in prayer, but also to form a prayer team that will regularly pray for the committee.

Nickerson lists ten mistakes search committees make when assessing pastoral candidates. While all these criteria don't apply to screening interim candidates, they are still good guidelines toward finding a good match. This next section will deal with more general criteria while the subsequent section will hone in on skills specific to intentional interim ministers.

Mistake #1: Not Differentiating Between a Call, Passion, and Competencies

Business consultant Robert Half says in his blog, "The costs of a bad hire are great and could have been prevented if those hiring did a more effective job of determining what kind of person they needed to accomplish the goals they desired."[2] A search committee's first job is to enter a season of prayer to determine what they want to accomplish during the interim time. Do they need a generalist who will do an effective job of leading them through a time of self-evaluation and goal setting? Do they need someone with skills in dealing with conflict or helping a congregation communicate more effectively? Do they want to revisit their organizational structure, boost their stewardship program, or do more community outreach?

While a call to ministry includes that intuitive, subjective whisper of God that this is to be one's vocation, it is not just a personal decision. A call must be tested and confirmed by the people of God, the church. John told the church in his day, "Don't believe every spirit, but test the spirits to see if they are from God" (1 John 4: 1). In Acts 13: 1–3, the leaders of the church were fasting and praying for guidance when the Holy Spirit said to them, "'Set apart for me Barnabas and Saul for the work to which I have called them.' Then after fasting and praying they laid their hands on them and sent them off." It is the church in a spirit of receptivity and discernment who confirms a call to ministry.

A call also includes gifts and graces that the pastor brings to ministry. Are they a person of prayer? Do people feel like the pastor ushers them into the presence of God? Are they effective at leading meetings, getting people to work together, and inspiring a vision for the future? What are the pastor's spiritual gifts?

So when looking for a pastor, whether interim or settled, be sure to have a sense of the skills, gifts, and competencies you are looking for to guide you through the time of transition. The author of Proverbs puts it bluntly, "Like an archer who wounds everyone, so is he who hires a fool, or hires those who pass by" (Proverbs 26: 10).

Mistake #2: Depending Too Much on the Interview to Evaluate a Candidate

Research shows that the typical interview increases the chances of choosing the best candidate by less than 2 percent. Conducting background checks, interviewing references and those not on the reference list (such as chairs of key committees), and hearing the candidate teach or preach (or lead a meeting) are other steps to consider. The most common interview blunders include not planning the interview carefully before it happens, using an interviewer who lacks experience, and being blinded by the personality or charisma of the candidate and therefore failing to evaluate performance.

Mistake #3: Using Successful People as Your Model and Standard

Beware of the "spiritual super hero" syndrome and the unfair and unrealistic comparisons that search committees make between the candidates they are interviewing and popular pastors or thriving churches. Confirm the skills and successes your candidates possess on their own merits and not compared to so-called superstars. Ask whether they best match the position you're trying to fill. Success in one setting doesn't necessarily mean it's transferable to another. The H. R. Chally Group did a study of one thousand sales superstars from seventy different companies and they found that the three most common characteristics of those high achievers were also the most common traits of the least successful performers in the same companies![3]

Mistake #4: Having Too Many Criteria

Identify no more than three to four criteria for the position. The committee should ask itself: What are our nonnegotiables? What are the key factors we are looking for? What are the deal-breakers for which a candidate would be automatically eliminated?

Mistake #5: Evaluating Personality Instead of Competency

Personality tests are wonderful for self-awareness but not for hiring. Many churches settle for personality because it is easier to see than competency and skills. Determining these takes more time and energy, but it is worth it. Churches are right to want pastors who are personable, compassionate, kind, and good-humored. Those qualities need not come at the expense of someone who has the ability to lead you toward your goals.

Mistake #6: Relying on Instincts to Spot Good Candidates

A search team can unconsciously project personal experiences and preferences onto a candidate and rely on a gut feeling that this person is the right one. This skews the assessment by placing more emphasis on subjective feeling rather than established criteria, background checks, and competencies.

Mistake #7: Overreliance on the "Good Guy" Criteria

Being a good person does not guarantee success in a particular setting. Theological compatibility, a good sense of humor, or similar cultural background doesn't equal competence. Nor is a pastor whom the committee has known for a long time, whether currently on the congregation's staff or from a nearby church, necessarily the right or best person for the job.

Mistake #8: Rushing the Decision-Making Process

This mistake could mean that there is no clear procedure for evaluation, nor a checklist of core competencies needed. Scrapping procedures and criteria when someone suddenly becomes available or because the search committee is getting tired can lead to mistakes. The result may be calling someone "who'll do" and not a candidate who people are excited about and who they think can do the job well.

Mistake #9: Bypassing the Reference Check

If the committee is wowed by a candidate, they may be tempted to skip the reference checks. Confirm all the information provided by a candidate, get criminal and financial background checks, and make sure you contact all references and talk to leaders from the church who aren't references.

Mistake #10: Failing to Include the Spouse or Partner in the Process

Including the family in the interview process is not only a courtesy but is essential in getting a comprehensive snapshot of the candidate. The lack of the support of a spouse or partner can be a deal-breaker. This is usually not done while looking for an interim pastor, but it is a courtesy to inquire about the candidate's spouse or partner, especially if the candidate is going to commute a long distance and stay over several nights a week.

TRAINING, SKILLS, AND EXPERIENCE NEEDED FOR INTERIM MINISTRY

The above list of ten potential mistakes search committees make when looking for a pastor or interim pastor are broad principles. Hiring an intentional interim pastor requires looking at additional criteria. There are three things in particular that you should look for: training, skills, and experience. The Interim Ministry Network (IMN) is the principal organization for training interim ministers. IMN has been training interim ministers for over thirty years and has regularly updated the curriculum according to feedback from participants, new needs discovered with local churches, new insights from the fields of organizational development and the social sciences, and the changing landscape of the American religious scene. Today, the IMN has over twelve hundred members from a wide scope of Protestant denominations and Judaism.

As noted in chapter 2, there are three tracks of training—Fundamentals of Transitional Ministry: The Work of the Leader; Fundamentals of Transitional Ministry: The Work of the Congregation; and Field Work. Once all three tracks are completed, participants are well prepared to be an intentional interim minister.

The Work of the Leader, a three-day training, helps a pastor discern whether interim ministry is best suited for him or her. The training helps him think about his temperament, skills, experience, and sense of call. In addition to learning how the Bible informs and guides the transitional time, participants learn three theories of organizational development that help them understand a church culture and work within it. Process tasks, the stages that an interim pastor walks through as she enters a new pastoral setting, are the core of the training. They include

- *Joining the Congregation*—understanding how it operates, seeing how leadership is exercised, and discovering the congregation's "style";
- *Focusing on What Needs to Be Done*—determining priorities and setting goals with the leadership team;

- *Analyzing the Congregational System*—using tools such as church life cycle theory and looking at the congregation through four lenses: identity (who are you?), context (what are the settings within and outside of the church that influence it?), process (how are things done?), and program (what do you do?);
- *Making Connections* with the denomination, the community, and the ecumenical and interfaith community; and lastly,
- *Evaluating the Ministry and Exiting Well.*

The next track is The Work of the Congregation. This is an intense five-day training that equips the interim with the biblical insights, tools, and concepts to help her lead a congregation through a fruitful interim stint. Participants learn about power relationships in congregations, managing differences and conflict, helping a congregation understand their heritage and how it impacts the church today, guiding a congregation to discover their core values and God's mission and vision for them, promoting stewardship, enhancing governance, and developing leaders, among many topics covered in the training. Adult learning models are used, involving a combination of lecture and discussion, small groups, case studies, and video presentations.

The third track is a field education project that focuses on one of the five process tasks of the three-day training or one of the five focus points of the five-day training. Each participant is part of a cohort of six to eight colleagues who design projects. On a monthly conference call, each participant will present his or her project and in turn receive feedback from colleagues. They then field test the project with a congregation and evaluate the outcomes and successes of the design. Projects have included the following:

- Assist congregational leaders to be free of the past in order to create openness to the future.
- Assist congregation to address mission and vision for the future.
- Assist congregation in developing leaders through a spiritual gifts assessment.
- Develop a comprehensive planning process to generate new identity, dreams, and vision.
- Broaden congregation's concept of stewardship beyond money to include time and talents.

- Develop faith-centered concept of leadership and offer leadership training to raise up new leaders to replace those who are burned out or unable to continue.
- Assist leaders in learning more effective ways to address conflict in the congregation.

After the participant has finished the field project and completed the evaluation and reflection piece, he or she is then given a certificate of completion of the three tracks of training. After completing the course there is an opportunity to become a Professional Transitional Specialist (PTS). This designation identifies those interim ministers who, in addition to completing the three tracks of training, verify formal academic work they have done, particularly in a specialty such as coaching, consulting, or work in family systems theory.

Applicants must verify at least two years of hands-on transitional ministry experience and submit a letter of good standing from their denomination. Every three years an updated resume of relevant continuing education must be submitted.

Several denominations such as the Presbyterian Church, USA, or the Evangelical Lutheran Church of America offer their own training that uses many of the same concepts as the IMN training. The Center for Congregational Health in Winston-Salem, North Carolina, is a collaborative partner with IMN and they developed the curriculum together. The Clergy Leadership Institute offers training using appreciative inquiry as the theoretical base of its model.[4] This training complements that of IMN.

To have an effective time of transitional ministry together, it is essential to select an interim minister with the appropriate training and a good sense of the impact the changing landscape of American religion has on local churches.

Training is important, but so are the skills and experience necessary to be an effective transitional pastor. Moreover, qualities of character, leadership, self-awareness, and integrity are crucial when hiring an interim specialist. IMN has identified the following skills as essential. They suggest the interim needs to have demonstrated proficiency in the following areas:[5]

- Making a quick, positive, and informed entry into the congregation's system
- Applying family systems learnings as a self-defined, nonanxious presence
- Helping the congregation to analyze its structure, history, and management
- Helping the congregation to identify its strengths for ministry and assist the congregation to recognize and address its dysfunctions
- Understanding the dynamics of change/maintenance in a congregation and assisting them to establish strategic goals and vision
- Recognizing and responding appropriately to conflict issues in the congregation

In addition, a person who serves the church as a transitional pastor should also have the following:[6]

- Education at the level required to meet the denomination's standards for ministerial standing
- Recognition or standing in a duly recognized denomination or church body
- Experience in planning and leading worship and preaching the Gospel
- Experience in at least two congregations in a leadership role with written performance evaluations available
- Special training that deals with congregational dynamics, the process of organizational transition, developmental tasks of the interim period, planning, human relations, group dynamics, consulting interventions, and church management
- Demonstrated ability to work effectively with volunteers in a church setting
- Pastoral training that includes helping people deal with grief, anger, and conflict, as well as pastoral care and counseling
- Administrative competency in church management, communication, planning, corporate decision making, negotiation, and mediation

IMN has also identified the following personal qualities and characteristics as important for transitional pastors to possess:[7]

- Clear sense of calling to the practice of transitional ministry
- A life of prayer
- Good ego strength: secure, mature, and emotionally stable
- Clear personal boundaries
- Action/goal oriented
- Flexible and adaptable
- Patient, empathetic, and understanding
- Effective level of physical and emotional vitality
- Sound, positive, and growing faith
- Ability to maintain an optimistic attitude
- Good sense of humor
- Commitment to continuing education in the field of professional transitional ministry

When you hire an interim pastor, the position should include a formal agreement or covenant between all parties, including clear statements regarding

- Position and expectations (goals) for the interim period with clear statements of who is responsible for given tasks
- Relationship of the intentional interim pastor to lay leadership and the search process, as well as to self-study and planning, recognizing that congregational self-study is more valuable when conducted prior to commencing the search for new leadership
- Skills, abilities, and preparation expected of the interim pastor
- Work hours and leave time
- Housing arrangements
- Compensation and benefits
- Specific agreement that the interim pastor will not be a candidate and will not be considered for the permanent position in the church he or she is serving as the interim
- Provision for Mutual Ministry Review and exit interview

A sample covenant-contract is included in appendix D.

Experience is the third criterion for an effective interim minister. You want to hire a person who has served in real live pastoral settings as a settled pastor and as an interim minister. An interim minister needs to be tested as a spiritual leader and practitioner of pastoral duties.

Almost all denominations require at least several years of parish ministry before a minister is assigned an interim position. IMN requires at least two years and suggests having served in two parishes before engaging in interim ministry. Rarely will a denomination ordain someone for interim ministry as a specialist or calling before they have served as a settled pastor. While it may indeed be a future calling, most Protestant denominations want the ordinand to experience life in a church setting to learn about the practice of ministry before going into interim ministry. Only then will ministers begin to understand the different roles a pastor plays in each setting.

You can see the skills of a candidate for interim ministry on his or her resume or in the profile that is unique to each denomination. There you will find the number of settled and interim positions the candidate has served, and the training he or she has received—academic, interim ministry training, and any workshops or continuing education. The candidate may have had specialized training in conflict management, grief counseling, or spiritual direction.

In addition, checking references is essential to get the full scope of a candidate. In written references people often tell about the character and personal qualities of the pastor, but they will also mention some of the programs, projects, and transitional tasks he did with the congregation. This will be a good indicator of the pastor's skill set. Phone interviews are essential to have in addition to the written references.

Interim ministers also have specialties that can be key for churches going through a unique transition time. You may have lost your property or had it severely damaged due to a tornado, flood, or hurricane. There are interim ministers who are specialists in helping congregations deal with the trauma a natural disaster leaves behind. Or perhaps your congregation has just gone through a serious conflict. Often it's over a pastor who lost favor with a segment of the congregation that led a charge to have him reviewed. Some were against him, some were for him, and the rest of the congregation was appalled at how their fellow Christians were treating the pastor and one another.

Some interim ministers who are specialists in conflict management and resolution can help heal an open wound. Or perhaps there has been clergy misconduct, whether sexual, financial, or abuse of power. Some interim ministers specialize in what is called "after pastor" situations where a clergy person has betrayed a sacred trust and people are feeling deeply angry and disenchanted. They are trained to lead people through a process that allows them to vent, work through, and reconcile difficult emotions and come to a place of acceptance and healing. Or maybe a church is wrestling with a decision about whether to struggle on or to close. Some interim ministers are specialists in helping congregations discern whether it's time to close, merge, or make a bold decision to do something new. If the decision is to close, the interim can help the congregation grieve, find hope in the midst of loss, and release their assets in meaningful ways to future generations.

Some interim ministers have specialized experience in stewardship, reorganizing governance structures, spiritual formation, helping congregations to discern purpose, mission, vision and strategic planning, and creative worship, just to name a few. Don't be afraid to inquire of your judicatory official about what kind of specialists might be available for your unique situation.

Not every church can afford a full-time interim minister nor might they have the need for one because of the size of the congregation. There's also the possibility that no trained or experienced interim pastor lives nearby or is willing to travel a long distance. This is a situation that might require some flexibility and creativity.

One option would be to hire a local pastor to lead worship, preach, offer the sacraments, and provide pastoral care. The church might hire an interim consultant who could have an initial face-to-face with the leadership to explain how he or she could assist in their process via conference calls or Skype. This might be a monthly call with intermediate conversations with the chair of the transition team or whatever body that was selected to either hire an interim or guide the in-between time. This person would coach you through the focus points you need to concentrate on and teach you how to gather information, talk about dreams for the future, conduct a survey, or address specific issues with which you are wrestling.

Another option would be to hire an intentional interim minister to work with a cluster of churches who are in a transitional time. You could find out from your judicatory official whether there are enough churches relatively close together who could benefit from such coaching or consulting. They wouldn't even need to be from the same denomination. The common denominator would be that you are all between pastors and need some help. This would be particularly helpful for small churches, isolated churches, or churches in rural or urban settings.

By now you're probably thinking even Moses or Jesus couldn't fit this bill. It goes without saying that all pastors, no matter how skilled or experienced, have feet of clay. We are "wounded healers," as Henri Nouwen put it. Paul reminds us that "we have this treasure in clay jars, so that it may be made clear that this extraordinary power belongs to God and does not come from us" (2 Corinthians 4: 7). By doing due diligence and trusting the Holy Spirit to guide the process, however, you can have a fruitful and joyous time during a transitional period in the life of your church.

QUESTIONS FOR REFLECTION AND DISCUSSION

1. What was the most important thing you learned from this chapter?
2. What do you value most about the four areas of effectiveness for an interim minister: training, skills, character, or experience?
3. What areas in the life of your church might require the special skills, training, and experience of an interim pastor? What are they and how might he or she help?
4. How could your church benefit from a full-time intentional interim minister? Given your particular circumstances, might there be another model that would be better for you? If so, what would be more helpful?

5

WHAT WILL WE DO?

The interval between pastors is not a time to coast or mark time. Nor is the interim pastor there to simply to fill an empty pulpit. There is a lot of work to do. Like all pastors, full-time interim pastors will provide

- Sunday worship leadership and preaching
- Pastoral care, visitation, and hospital visits
- Counsel to your boards and committees (vestry, session, deacons—whatever the terminology of your denomination is) to guide the life and ministry of the congregation
- Teaching skills for adult education classes and confirmation classes if that is an expectation of the pastor
- Administrative work including supervision of other staff persons
- Staff support for programs and committees of the congregation
- Participation in denominational, ecumenical, and interfaith gatherings

Part-time interim pastors will only be able to do three or four items on the list.

In addition, an interim minister leads a congregation through the transition time after an installed pastor has departed, helping the congregation discover who they are, celebrate what they do well, experiment with new methods and ministries, and getting them ready to welcome the leadership of a new installed pastor. Interim ministers understand the dynamics of a congregation in transition, including feelings of grief, loss, and, sometimes, relief or anger. There is often some anxiety, nervousness, and turbulence. If a church does not have a behavioral covenant, as discussed in chapter 3, this would be a good task to undertake shortly after the interim minister has arrived.

Next, the interim minister and the congregation enter a mutually agreeable covenant that spells out the expectations, goals, and desired outcomes of their time together. While there are no cookie-cutter approaches, for each congregation is unique, there are principles and practices of transitional ministry that are useful for churches who want to use the time together to the maximum benefit. Compensation is based on the package of the last pastor or the anticipated compensation package for the next pastor, and is determined by the amount of time expected (full time or part time).

One of the first tasks of an interim pastor is to establish a transition team. A transition team works closely with the interim minister to accomplish the transitional ministry tasks described below and to interpret the congregation to the pastor. They function like a tour guide when visiting a new country. Things they can help the interim pastor understand include the traditions, habits, and norms of the congregation and what kind of events they will best respond to that will stimulate participation and conversation. The team will also help set up various gatherings and discussion groups to discern the congregation's history, strengths, and growing edges, and the type of pastoral leadership that is needed to bring them into the future.

It is best to have people on the transition team who represent the various demographic groups of the congregation (age, gender, perspectives, newcomer, longevity, and so forth). It is critical that this task force consist of people who can listen well and share feedback from the congregation accurately. It is best to avoid people who come with heavy agendas and can't listen. People with a good reputation in the church, decent organizational skills, and an ability to communicate to a wide range of people are best suited.

This entire process is based on the belief that the Spirit is alive and well in your congregation and that as a church you can discern that Spirit and the direction God is calling the church. Jesus promised that "When the Spirit of truth comes, he will guide you into all the truth; for he will not speak on his own, but will speak whatever he hears, and he will declare to you the things that are to come" (John 16: 14). I have a colleague who says that a vision is formed when we "find out what God is already doing and get on board!"

Some of the tasks of the transition team include

- Meeting regularly for six to nine months and praying for each other and the congregation.
- Designing, advertising, and implementing all-church meetings that help gather data and facilitate conversation around Who are we? Who is our Neighbor? And What is God calling us to do and be?
- Listening to and feeding back to the congregation what is being shared.
- Facilitating a series of small focus groups and interview teams that meet in people's homes to sharpen the focus of the information gathered at all church functions and to reach those who are no longer able to be active in church.
- Pulling together all the information/perspectives gathered and writing a summary with suggested actions for the congregation to discuss and act upon. This information will be invaluable to a search committee as they draft a church profile to circulate to pastoral candidates. In some cases, the transition team writes the first draft of the church profile.

Sometimes a congregational survey is an effective way to get information, but there should be some rules. First, surveys must be signed and not anonymous. There are no anonymous Christians; we all have names. Surveys are not trash cans where everyone gets to say nasty or mean things about the pastor, leaders, or the church without being accountable.

Second, there should always be discussion and feedback with small groups about the survey results. For instance, if a questionnaire asks, "On a scale of 1 to 10 how would you rate our worship service?" And the average response was 7. What does that mean? What can a pastor or leadership team or director of music do with that information without a conversation? They would like to know, "What worship services are the strongest?" "Why?" "What elements of worship put you into the presence of God?" "What would you like more of? Less of?" and so on. If questions are ranked on a continuum it is best to use criteria such as

Strongly Agree, Agree, Not Sure, Disagree, or Strongly Disagree with an opportunity to write comments.

A good resource for congregational surveys is Holy Cow! Consulting. They have an excellent product called the Congregational Assessment Tool (CAT).[1] CAT is a customizable assessment instrument that can help a congregation and its leaders to

- Measure the level of satisfaction and energy in the congregation
- Identify the critical success factors for improving organizational climate
- Pinpoint the strengths of the congregation's culture
- Discover where members would like to go in the future
- Gauge readiness for change
- Uncover potential resources they may be missing
- Prepare for a search for the next pastor or priest

This is an affordable, extremely useful assessement that can be conducted online, and Holy Cow! will interpret it for you.

Another resource is from the Hartford Institute for Religious Research, which is part of the Hartford Theological Seminary. They make available three Congregational Assessment Inventories: the Pastoral Search Inventory, the Church Planning Inventory, and the Parish Profile Inventory.[2] They can conduct and interpret the survey online (which is far easier and preferable) or you can distribute and collate it yourself. The downside of this inventory is that it is very long and some people have a hard time finishing it. Regardless, research both of these options and see which one might work best for you.

FIVE FOCUS POINTS THAT GUIDE THE TRANSITION PROCESS

Once the transition team is in place and they are clear on their job description, the interim minister will train and guide them as they lead the congregation through what are called focus points. The focus points are not linear tasks that need to be completed sequentially. Neither do each of them require the same amount of attention. The priorities and the attention given to some focus points more than others is determined by the needs of each congregation. The five focus points are heritage, leadership, mission, connections, and future.

Heritage

Heritage includes many factors that influence congregational identity and self-understanding. Issues of identity include the core values, bedrock beliefs, local history, denominational and theological heritage, and local and world events.

Core values are in many ways more important than a mission or vision statement. Core values are the gunpowder that fires the bullet of mission. Through a variety of different exercises, churches may learn that things like spiritualty, mission, respect, traditions, acceptance, integrity, prayer, and so on are at the heart of who they are as a congregation. Those values shape their mission and calling. For example, if a strong core value is caregiving and the congregation thinks they should do social action, there may be a disconnect between what they think they should do and what they actually have passion for. The difference is between what the church's head tells them to do and what their heart tells them to do. There is an exercise in appendix E called "What Do We Have Energy For?" that helps congregations assess what they have a passion for.

Bedrock beliefs, as noted in chapter 3, are those nonnegotiable principles that define a church's relationship with God, one another, and the world. These are not so much doctrinal standards as they are practices. For instance, a bedrock belief might be "God answers prayer," "God supports us during trials," or "a true Christian gives sacrificially." These may be latent beliefs and core values that yield an aha moment when they are formally identified. In other words, they make sense; yes, we knew that's who we were, but we never named them as such.[3]

History includes key events and memories in the life of the church. It could be building projects, notable pastors, significant ministries and accomplishments, and controversy. It is a time to examine when we were at our best and when we became rather nasty. Examining those moments gives insight into how the church responds under duress.

History also includes personal history such as significant times during worship when God was palpably present—communion on Christmas Eve, a mission trip to Mexico, when my child was baptized, or when I buried my father at this church. These events are in turn laid upon local and national events. It could be when GE left the community and many became jobless, or when many young men were conscripted during the Vietnam War. These events shape a congregation in both discernable and indiscernible ways.

Finally, how and under what circumstances the church was founded impacts the identity and sense of self of a congregation. In their book *Energizing the Congregation*, Carl Dudley and Sally Johnson convincingly advance the thesis that churches have self-images that shape their ministry.[4] After studying over one hundred congregations in eighteen different denominations, these keen observers of church dynamics found five images consistently emerging. Although individual churches do not fit neatly into all the criteria or types they describe, there are certain observable patterns. The five images they discerned were churches as survivor, prophet, pillar, pilgrim, and servant.

Survivor Churches move from crisis to crisis yet still survive: the boiler blows, they have a string of short-term pastors, or the manufacturing firm that sustained the economic life of the community moves elsewhere. Like the proverbial cat, they always seem to land on their feet but with one less life left. Not surprisingly, survivor churches are primarily located in transient, declining, aging, urban neighborhoods, with widespread social, familial, and economic upheaval. Perseverance is the watchword for these congregations.

Prophet Churches are what we usually describe as "social action churches." A common commitment to confront evil in social structures, corporations, governments, and institutions draws the membership of these churches together. They often initiate action against what they perceive as destructive or unjust to persons or communities, and they tend to be high-commitment churches.

Pillar Churches sense a unique responsibility to a geographical community, whether to a neighborhood or an entire town. It is rightly described as an institution of the geographical setting. The architecture may indicate the type of church this is. It could be the sole white-pillared church in a rural community or a large stone gothic structure in an urban center. They have names like Old North or First Church. Like the building, the members are pillars in the community—teachers, selectmen and women, members of the town meeting, and persons active in the high school scholarship drive. Pillar churches tend to have polished, traditional worship services and are homogeneous in culture, race, economic standing, and ethnic or national group.

Pilgrim Churches are rooted in a *people* and a tradition. Many pilgrim congregations began as immigrant churches that welcomed people from the "home country"—Italy, Germany, Poland, Vietnam, and hosts of others. Embracing a strong "pilgrim theology," as wanderers looking for a homeland, pilgrim churches may assist new groups of immigrants from different ethnic backgrounds to establish new churches. The church dwells where the people dwell and sustains them as a community of faith while they assimilate into a new culture.

Servant Churches focus on the needs of individuals in quiet, modest ways. Members of these churches will visit shut-ins, send cards to the sick, and take meals to new families or the bereaved. Their service is extremely practical. They live their faith in simple service through supportive and pastoral ministries. The pastors of these churches tend to be caring shepherds who encourage and nurture their congregants in their care for others. They can also be called Golden Rule churches.

Churches, like individuals, have personalities and a self-image, a way of perceiving and understanding themselves.

Leadership

The second focus point is leadership. A change of pastoral leadership often precipitates changes in the lay leadership as well. Former leaders may take a less active role while new persons become more involved. Many congregations address their internal leadership needs during the interim time. Here's an opportunity to teach and help people develop leadership skills.

Jesus is the model of what we call "servant leadership."[5] In the Upper Room the night before his execution, Jesus stood up (as when he left eternity and came among us), took off his outer garment (as when Jesus put aside his divinity and took up our humanity), knelt down, and washed his disciples' feet (a stunning act of humility from one who is the Son of God and truly an example of what "new humanity" looks like).

> "Do you know what I have done to you?" Jesus asked. "You call me
> Teacher and Lord—and you are right, for that is what I am. So if I,

your Lord and Teacher, have washed your feet, you also ought to wash one another's feet. For I have set you an example that you also should do as I have done to you." (John 13: 12–15)

Genuine leaders are those who seek to serve others, build up the body of Christ, and do not self-aggrandize.

A review of the effectiveness of leaders and how they are chosen is also an important step in this focus point. Good questions to ask are: are there places where one person or groups of people have too much authority and power without the commensurate accountability? How can you balance experience with energy and innovative ideas? Are there leaders or staff members who are entrenched and need to move on? This focus point also looks at infrastructure to see if current structures best support ongoing ministries. Is the structure of the church too cumbersome for leaders to do their jobs most effectively? Could their time be put to better use than attending many meetings? Do the bylaws require more people than necessary to support the work of the church? What would make people excited about being on a leadership team?

Kennon Callahan, in his book *Twelve Keys to an Effective Church*, dedicates a chapter to the characteristics of effective leaders.[6] He lists the following ten characteristics.

- Competencies and skills that match well with the job.
- General competencies in work patterns.
- Compassion in human relationships.
- Commitment to the specific leadership position.
- Commitment to the congregation.
- Commitment to the church's mission in the world.
- Ability to function well during good times.
- Ability to function well in stress and conflict situations.
- Solid reputation and functioning in prior groups.
- Strong personal character, integrity, and self-esteem.

Callahan's concern is that churches often put people in leadership positions because the members are so committed, but they don't have the competencies (the ability to get things done well and in a timely manner) or skills needed to do the job well. Competency is more important than commitment. This is not being cruel, but recognizing that some people have the gifts and graces better suited for another ministry.

There are eleven areas that should also be considered during the transitional time when exploring current practices of selecting, organizing, and building patterns of healthy, effective leadership.

No. 1: Shifts of Power. When a pastor leaves and an interim arrives, there are often shifts in power. Some people will step down and others will rush to fill a vacuum. Conflicts may occur as people attempt to balance power or to change the balance of power. Some individuals may try to gain specific leadership roles. Consequently, the congregation needs to deal with the overall issue of leadership. There may be few leaders available. Leaders may need specific training and priorities may need to be set regarding where and how leaders should be used. Negotiating power is always a dynamic in churches, but during the interim period they often surface with more urgency.

No. 2: Review of Position Descriptions. The interim time presents an opportunity to assure that job descriptions are current so there is no confusion about how people and committees are to function and what is expected of them. Are there job descriptions in place not only for staff, but also for board and committee members and chairs? If so, when was the last time they were reviewed and updated? These should include not only a list of duties and qualifications, but also skill sets needed to do the job, including training and support provided, and the person to whom each one reports. Put the revision date on it as well. Requirements for temperament is also necessary when writing a job description. For instance, don't write, "Answer the phone and route it to the appropriate staff member," but "Answer the phone in a friendly and professional manner and route it to the appropriate staff member." This yardstick will measure not only the performance of the task but also the quality of the performance.

No. 3: Policies and Procedures Review. Does each board and committee have a notebook of their policies and procedures, which includes dates for annual events with a punch list of what needs to be done in preparation, where records are kept and items are stored, and helpful resources that can be passed on to new chairs and members? Does it need to be updated? Is there a punch list of when and how things are to proceed for annual events?

No 4: Worshipful Work. Do boards and committees see themselves as intentional, spiritual communities? Is time given in meetings for Bible study, a devotional, mutual sharing and support, and prayer? Or do they begin with a perfunctory prayer and then work through the agenda? Spiritual practices build up groups working together and remind them that they are not doing "church work," but the "work of the church."

No. 5: Evaluations. When were staff evaluations last done? Is there a procedure in place? Are there rewards or penalties for good or poor job performance? Evaluations are to be mutual based upon the mission, vision, and goals of the congregation. The best evaluations are "mutual ministry" evaluations that do not focus on the pastor or staff but on the whole ministry of the church, including the leaders and the congregation.

No. 6: Conflicts of Interests in Your Bylaws or Other Documents. Do members of the same household sit on a board or committee and both have a vote? Is an officer or staff member also a member of the church? Are there conflicts of interest with that arrangement? Are there rules about hiring people from within the congregation for contract work or at least requiring them to submit a bid?[7]

No. 7: Personnel Manual. This would be an appropriate time to have any human resource professionals in your congregation put a manual together that would lay out vacation time, days off, personal leave, dispute settlement, evaluation procedures, sexual harassment policies, and more.

No. 8: Staff and Committee Members' Skill Sets. Interim ministry can be a time to help some people gracefully step down. This can be done by reviewing the job description to make sure it supports the work of the church and that the person has the necessary skills to perform the job. For instance, if the job requires the employee to have facility with Microsoft Office and they are unwilling to receive training for it that is an indicator that the person does not have the requisite skills to do the job. This is also a time to encourage newer/younger members to step up.

No. 9: Nominating Committee Process. Does the nominating committee just plug holes to fill slots or is there a system in place to help people recognize and use their spiritual gifts? Are people placed in positions they are passionate about? Is the number of people required by the bylaws to fill committees realistic? Does the current organizational structure need to be evaluated and changed to meet present-day realities of people's time and other commitments?[8]

No. 10: Leadership Development Training. Help leaders understand the church as an emotional system and what constitutes a healthy leader. Provide training on writing an effective agenda and running a good meeting. Does each board or committee chair have a vision for their committee that supports the overall mission of the church? Are the members of the committee on board with the vision?

No. 11: Boundaries. Do people observe boundaries appropriate to their role, office, or assignment in the church? Is access to relationships, information, and decisions limited to only those on boards and committees? Are relationships among members honored with honesty and integrity, without keeping secrets or sabotaging each other's work or personhood? Is confidential information repeated indiscriminately with other members of the congregation? When boards and committees make decisions appropriate to its authority and according to the rules and roles of the system, do church members abide by those decisions? Do any informal groups or individuals have the power to overrule legitimate actions taken by boards and committees? To what extent do members know that their concerns will be received and heard by a board or committee and that the board will consider their concerns in light of the whole church, even if it does not do what a particular member wants it to do? Is the office of the pastor respected and is he or she treated with civility and respect?

Mission

This third focus point looks closely at defining and redefining a sense of purpose and direction of a congregation. The term is meant to be understood broadly, as the overarching raison d'être of a church. Underneath this umbrella, a congregation will refine this focus point by reflecting upon and writing a purpose statement, a mission, a vision, and a plan.

A Purpose Statement is a precise statement about why you exist. It captures succinctly why an organization exists and what it does. It should be brief, concise, and memorable. It is the elevator speech you would give someone if they asked, "Tell me about your church." In a few sentences, could you tell this questioner why you exist and what you are called to do and be? Kellogg's purpose statement, for instance, is

"Nourishing families so they can flourish and thrive." A purpose statement must use words that have deep meaning for the congregation.

Below are some examples of purpose statements from various
churches:

Love God
Grow Together
Reach the World

A Place For Your Spirit

We Grow Human Hearts

Open Door: Welcome
Open Spirits: Spiritual Growth
Open Road: Mission
Open Table: Covenant and Communion

A *Mission Statement* (what you do) is a short statement describing
what an organization is called to do and is used to help guide decisions
about priorities, actions, and responsibilities. As noted previously, Peter
Drucker says the mission statement should answer the question: "What
business are you in?" The mission always comes first, says Drucker, and
should drive every other program and ministry. Drucker uses mission
here as I use purpose. The purpose of the church is changed lives.
When Drucker's insights are applied to a local congregaton the function
of management is to make the church more church-like, not the church
more business-like. (What if, for instance, our boards and committees
became small groups for spiritual formation?)

The best mission statements are clear, memorable, and concise.
Most church mission statements are often way too long to remember,
too general to be meaningful, and lack clarity and focus. These are a few
examples of good mission statements:

> *The Riverside Church in the City of New York seeks to be a commu-
> nity of faith. Its members are united in the worship of God known in
> Jesus, the Christ, through the inspiration of the Holy Spirit. The
> mission of the Church is to serve God through word and witness; to
> treat all human beings as sisters and brothers; and to foster respon-
> sible stewardship of all God's creation.*

Seeking to put God's love into action, Habitat for Humanity brings people together to build homes, communities and hope.

To lead people worldwide into a growing relationship with Jesus Christ and to strengthen the local church.

We believe all people matter to God and that Christ's message and ministry through the local church is the hope of the world.

When looking at mission, it is helpful to understand that mission functions at three distinct levels: the macro, micro, and method level. The first is your macro mission. The macro mission is that list of classic, universal functions for churches of every size, in every generation, and in every kind of community. In the Bible, it comes down to two, the Great Commandment and the Great Commission. The Great Commandment is how the church should be: "You shall love the Lord your God with all your heart, soul, mind and strength and your neighbor as yourself" (Matthew 22: 36–40). So here are two nonnegotiables: love of God and love of neighbor.

The Great Commission is what the church should do. "Go, therefore, teaching others to observe all that I have taught you, baptizing them in the name of the Father, and of the Son, and of the Holy Spirit. And behold, I am with you always even to the end of the age" (Matthew 28: 16–20). So there are three other nonnegotiables: Go—do and tell about God's love revealed in Jesus, teach people about the ways of God, and baptize and make committed disciples.

The next level is your micro mission—this is what your particular congregation is called to do and be. The micro mission answers the question: "How does First Community Church apply the macro mission to its unique setting with its givens?" It should include worship, caregiving, outreach and evangelism, Christian formation/education, and building community (Acts 2: 42–47). Why is the micro mission important? A healthy congregational mission identity fits its size, its members, its resources, and the needs of people in its surrounding community. A micro mission identity must fit a particular congregation, community, or demographics.

The third level is your method mission—these are the concrete, specific applications of the above to our place, time, and setting given our resources, people, and energy. The method mission answers the "how to" questions. How to do worship, how to do member care, how to do outreach, and so on. The macro and micro mission should always govern the answers to these questions and determine which best apply to the proposed ministry or program. You want to have a golf club? Fine, how does it help us love God and one another better? Is it the best thing to do or just a good thing? You want to have Vacation Bible School. Great! How does it help us go, teach, and disciple people in Christ's name? Is it a good thing to do or the best thing we can do to reach a given population? Every program, event, and project needs to pass the scrutiny of "does this fit with our purpose?"

A Vision Statement (desired end state) is a word picture of what your congregation would look like if it were, in fact, to fulfill its mission statement. It is a one-sentence statement describing the clear and inspirational long-term desired change resulting from the work of your congregation.

- It identifies what would be different if the church was faithful.
- It includes hints of the criteria by which the church will measure its ministry, describing what will be different about the church in three to five years.
- It draws a picture of a future that is sufficiently rich in detail to offer some direction and guidance for the trip.

Here are a few examples:

The Five Hallmarks of the Hills Church Vision

- *Fostering Authentic Relationships*
- *Deepening Our Spiritual Journeys*
- *Investing in Children and Youth*
- *Welcoming, Inviting and Involving Our Neighbors*
- *Caring for Others through Outreach*

As a community, we're devoted to building an engaged, passionate, spiritually healthy community of people that makes up Mars Hill. We're also devoted to engaging and impacting one another and others, believing that Jesus himself set an example of service and that we've been given the responsibility to follow it.

First Church—
Grounded in God,
Our hope and our healing
Growing in community,
With Jesus our center
Acting in love,
Made bold by the Spirit

Goals, Objectives, and Plans are where a church fleshes out its method mission. A saying I often use with churches is, "If you aim at nothing, you'll hit it every time." Churches are full of good intentions, but we know where that road leads. Often a team will put together a strategic plan, the leadership will endorse it, and it sits on the shelf until the next strategic plan is drawn up.

A plan, strategy, or blueprint, whatever you choose to call it, should be a living document that is visited at every governing board or leadership meeting to see how the congregation is doing with meeting its vision.

Goals state what the congregation and its leaders must commit themselves to do or to be in order to monitor the unique future being shaped. Objectives state how the congregation will accomplish those goals. Goals are often expressed by action plans: who will do what by when and at what costs. Objectives are SMART: specific, measurable, attainable/achievable, relevant, and time bound.[9] Focusing on the difference between what is and what is hoped for is called "gap theory planning."[10] The basic path of gap theory planning is to follow this sequence:

- Here's where we are now.
- Here's where we want or feel called to be in the future.
- Here's a description of the gap between where we are and where we want to be.
- Here's what we must learn to get there.
- Here are our recommendations and action plans to achieve our vision.

Business leaders, denominational leaders, nonprofit organizations, consultants, and others sometimes put vision before mission or objectives before goals. It really doesn't matter what you call them; the definitions and concepts don't change. The bottom line is a determination of your church's purpose and a plan to put meat on those bones.

Connections

The fourth focus point is connections. Connections are all the relationships and networks a faith community builds beyond itself including the denomination, community, and ecumenical and interfaith groups. This information can be gathered through demographic surveys, interviews with community leaders, and neighborhood walks observing what's going on Sunday mornings, what businesses have come and gone, and who is living in the neighborhood.

Have chats with those out working in their yard. Find out what's important to them. Where do they struggle? Do they have a faith community? If they were to try one, what would they be looking for? Try praying as you walk, either silently or out loud as a group. Ask God to help you to see what you need to see, to inspire insight and possible ways to engage and minister to your neighbors.

Future

The fifth and last focus point is preparing for the future. Sometimes churches think they need to come to terms with their past before they can move on. In some cases that may be true, but more important, they have to come to terms with their future. That is what they must prepare for and live into. The future is where God is pulling the universe. While keeping these truths before us, the transition team and church leadership also has to deal with the nitty gritty of calling the best pastor for the immediate future. Focusing on the future requires a healthy and honest assessment of the work done on the other focus points so that the congregation can turn its energy toward proactive decision making.

This focus point involves synthesizing the interim work done into a coherent narrative, selecting and training the pastoral search committee, and coaching the committee (as requested) to accomplish its work. This is almost always the work of the judicatory official rather than the interim pastor. Making certain a fair and just compensation package is in place and the goals and expectations of the search committee, congregation, and called pastor are the same is part of this work.

SPIRITUAL PRACTICES AND DISCERNMENT

While some might think this should be on top of the list of things a congregation needs to do during a transitional time (really, all the time!), I have put it last to underscore its importance during the whole process. As we've noted before, sometimes churches go on autopilot after many years of doing church the same way. They have lost their "mojo" and seem to just be going through the motions.

Spiritual mojo comes from the Holy Spirit. Before Jesus ascended to heaven he promised, "But you will receive *power* when the Holy Spirit comes on you; and you will be my witnesses in Jerusalem, and in all Judea and Samaria, and to the ends of the earth" (Acts 1: 8). The word for "power" in Greek is *dunamis. Dunamis* is not just any power; the word often refers to miraculous power or marvelous works, such as when Jesus perceived that power went out of him when a woman in a crowd touched his clothing (Mark 5: 30). The word can also refer to moral and spiritual power. Paul reminded his protégé Timothy of the spiritual energy God gives us. "For the Spirit God gave us does not make us timid, but gives us *power*, love and self-discipline" (2 Timothy 1: 7).

Spiritual practices during the interim time are essential to sustain this spiritual power. It promotes a healthy integration of spirituality and action. They reestablish or may even introduce ancient and ever-contemporary practices that ground a congregation in their essential purpose: to praise God, proclaim the Gospel of Jesus Christ, and to remain open to the urgings of the Holy Spirit. Spiritual practices can help churches get their mojo back.

Spiritual practices can include celebration, chastity, confession, fasting, fellowship, frugality, giving, guidance, hospitality, humility, intimacy, meditation, prayer, reflection, self-control, servanthood, service, silence, simplicity, singing, slowing, solitude, study, submission, surrender, teaching, and worship. This is an exhaustive list, which the historic church has practiced in various times and places. While many of these may be foreign to people in some mainline, historic churches, many can be learned and practiced.

Spiritual practices are best introduced through small groups because they allow for people to engage in the practice and then reflect upon it. A more intimate setting gives room for vulnerability and open sharing.

Fine books by Dorothy Bass (*Practicing Our Faith: A Way of Life for a Searching People*), Barbara Brown Taylor (*An Altar in the World: A Geography of Faith*), and Richard Foster (*Celebration of Discipline: The Path to Spiritual Growth*) are a great starting place.[11] Read a chapter a week, and assign a practice to the participants as homework until the next gathering.

Put together small groups that explore different styles and methods of prayer. Teaching and practicing these can be illuminating. The growing practice of *apophatic* prayer (listening) can be illuminating and uplifting for many. Centering prayer, meditation, *lectio divina* (praying with scripture), journaling, and walking the labyrinth are all forms of apophatic prayer. In one class, I led all of these styles plus built a wailing wall out of bricks where participants could put slips of paper with their hurts and wounds written on them. We looked at lamentation in the Prophets and Psalms even as they mourned their own laments and losses and placed them in God's hands.

Learning some of these practices in small groups may lead to spiritual and emotional healing, encourage forgiveness, and result in reconciliation. Practices build community and trust, teach prayer in its many forms, and encourage deep listening that results in discernment and confidence that God is indeed still speaking and has new paths for a community of faith to explore. One of the greatest benefits of engaging in spiritual practices is learning to accept yourself as God's beloved, which enables you to love others and to see them as fellow travelers on the Way.

Engaging in these activities can be life changing and enriching. Personal and group transformation may contribute to healthy and significant transformation for the whole congregation. Change can sometimes come in a dramatic fashion, such a Paul's conversion on the Damascus Road, but more often it is subtle and soulful. Spiritual growth almost always emerges through a divine birthing process.

Another teaching opportunity during a time of transition is helping people discover their spiritual gifts. As people discern God's gifts to them, they can feel empowered for ministry that fulfills them and blesses others. Engaging in spiritual disciplines during the interim time grounds both the pastor and people in the energy and peace of God. They are essential for revitalization, embracing oneself as God's beloved, and taking on a new sense of what it means to be a people of God.

QUESTIONS FOR REFLECTION AND DISCUSSION

1. One thing an interim minister can do is help a congregation look at things differently and from a different perspective. By reframing their current circumstances, churches might see some things they might not otherwise see. Go to appendix F and look at the graphics there. How do they change when you look at them closely? Do you see things you didn't see on your first look?
2. Of the five focus points, which do you think are most important for your church to look at?
3. How has your church welcomed new clergy?
4. Where do you expect there might be anxiety in your congregation? Excitement? Anticipation?
5. What kind of spiritual practices does your church already have? How open do you think people are in learning new ways to experience God and make decisions?

6

BUT WE LIKE THINGS
THE WAY THEY ARE

Spencer Johnson, a onetime physician who left his career to write books about life and business, including *The One-Minute Manager*, wrote a wildly popular book called *Who Moved My Cheese?*[1] Even though it was written eighteen years ago, it continues to be applicable to institutions experiencing change. Its brilliance was in its simplicity. The fable involves two mice, Scurry and Sniff, and two "little people," Hem and Haw, who live together in a maze. They are quite content because they have found a huge source of cheese, their favorite food. Hem and Haw have even moved their houses to be near it and it has become the center of their lives. But they do not notice that it is getting smaller and are devastated when they arrive at the site one morning and find the cheese is gone.

The mice foresaw this and they move on to discover more cheese. The humans didn't foresee this. Their overconfidence blinded them to the slowly dwindling supply. But they won't leave their section of the maze to look for more. They're afraid of what's out there in the maze. They have gotten used to their old ways. They have started to believe they were *entitled* to the cheese. Yet this only makes things worse, as their tenacious hanging on ensures that they will go hungry.

So they scream angrily, "WHO MOVED MY CHEESE?"

Hem and Haw decide to stay because they hope the cheese will show up there once again. They get bitter and blame everything and everyone but themselves. They complain that they worked hard to find the cheese and *deserve* more. After a long time, their situation hasn't changed; no new cheese has appeared. They continue to blame each other for their problems. They start using sophisticated tools to dig behind the walls because they think the cheese might be behind there.

Eventually, Hem gets smart and decides to explore the maze for more cheese. He tries to convince Haw to go with him, but he won't. Hem finds tiny bits of a new type of cheese in the maze, which he brings back to Haw. Haw refuses to eat it, because it's not like the old type of cheese. He would rather stick with what's familiar, even though it isn't satisfying, rather than risk something new.

Hem keeps exploring since these tiny bits aren't enough to sustain him. As he explores new areas of the maze, he pushes past his fears and learns many life lessons. He writes his insights on the wall from time to time to encourage himself to move on and to guide Haw, if he ever decides to follow him.

He finally finds a new place deep in the maze that has a ton of cheese, including all sorts of new types. There he meets Sniff and Scurry again, who have already been there for quite a while. He writes all the lessons he wrote earlier on a large wall:

- **Change Happens.** *They Keep Moving the Cheese.*
- **Anticipate Change.** *Get Ready for the Cheese to Move.*
- **Monitor Change.** *Smell the Cheese Often So You Know When It Is Getting Old.*
- **Adapt to Change Quickly.** *The Quicker You Let Go of Old Cheese, the Sooner You Can Enjoy New Cheese.*
- **Change.** *Move with the Cheese.*
- **Enjoy Change!** *Savor the Adventure and Enjoy the Taste of New Cheese!*
- **Be Ready to Change Quickly and Enjoy It Again.** *They Keep Moving the Cheese.*

The allegory well captures that moment after we have lost a job or a relationship and we believe it is the end of the world. Churches in decline or a shadow of their former selves may despair that they can revive. All the good things were in the past, and all the future holds is fear. Yet Johnson's message is that instead of seeing change as the end of something, we must learn to see it as a beginning. We know this instinctively, but we get stuck in a rut, and the familiar is most comfortable. To make himself accept reality, Haw writes this on the wall of the maze: "If you do not change, you can become extinct."

Thom Rainer, the president and CEO of LifeWay Christian Resources, uses the title of *Who Moved My Cheese?* as a springboard to his book about changes within churches called *Who Moved My Pulpit?*[2] The book begins by describing Derek, the seasoned pastor of a church of about 250 in the Midwest. He has seen an influx of millennials (those born between 1982 and 2004) attending worship, so he begins to use a more conversational, informal style of preaching. He gets a lot of positive feedback but is wise enough to know to proceed incrementally. So he preaches in his more formal style for four to six weeks and then offers a conversational sermon. Over time he more often than not preaches in his adopted chatty, storytelling method and becomes uncomfortable using the pulpit. It just doesn't fit his new style, so he removes it.

The outcry of emails, phone calls, parking lot conversations, Facebook postings, and finger-wagging scoldings that follow is merciless. One would have thought Pastor Derek had denied the Resurrection of Christ! This is almost worse. One Sunday morning when the pastor enters he sees huddled enclaves of people whispering among themselves. There is tension in the air. Then all of a sudden he notices the old pulpit is back! You can hear a paperclip drop when the pastor cries out, "Who moved my pulpit?!"

On one level, we know that a pulpit is only a lectern, a piece of furniture, perhaps made out of wood, from which to deliver a sermon. But it is a sacred piece of furniture. Objects become sacred because of what they represent. A pulpit is where the Word of God is read and expounded upon. A pulpit gives the pastor gravitas and authority. These meanings and associations are to be respected and honored and it is good to reflect upon why they are sacred. What gives this object meaning and stability? Do the symbols have the same meaning for everyone or are they a hindrance?

Interim pastors enter an environment where change has already occurred. The congregation feels like someone has moved their pulpit! Interim ministers, particularly in the early months, work more to stabilize the situation than to change it. In fact, intentional interim ministers are trained to manage change with care and caution, with discernment and deliberation. They are not entering your setting to "shake things up" for the sake of shaking things up, but to have the congregation get an honest and healthy take on itself. This self-understanding focuses on what is working well, what the church values, and how to do more of that.

In a world of constant change, many of us look to our church for stability and security. When a settled pastor leaves, that sense of sanctuary is disrupted as the changes that occur are felt in all aspects of church life. The changes may be met with a variety of emotions—grief, anger, frustration, surprise, relief, or hope. These reactions are a normal response to any time of transition. Sometimes the interim pastor can become the focus for this emotional energy. Some people may perceive the interim pastor as being the one to blame for "stirring the pot," when in fact, needed but stressful adjustments of the congregation's practices have surfaced. In addition, unresolved issues sometimes reemerge during the interim time. Confronting these issues can be difficult but necessary for the long-term effectiveness and mission of the congregation. A good interim minister cannot overlook opportunities to address issues that relate to the well-being of the church and its readiness for a new leader and a new ministry. The changes that might be indicated are not undertaken arbitrarily, but only with the support of the lay leadership of the church.

Rev. Kathleen C. Rolenz, a Unitarian Universalist interim minister, uses two helpful metaphors to describe interim/transitional tasks.[3] The first metaphor views the transition as soil, where solid ground is broken up to allow for seeds to take root. Transitional ministry is a time to plow new fields, break up clods of dried out soil, plant seeds, and see what will grow. The interim's job is to discern with the congregation what fields need to be overturned to permit new growth and vitality, and which ones need to lay fallow for now.

The second metaphor sees the church as a plant in need of pruning. Good pruning requires looking carefully at the plant, using sharp tools, and following practices that work best for a particular species. When plants are allowed to grow without pruning, they become "leggy," grow without discipline, and stop bearing fruit as they once did. Some programs that were started long ago, maybe by a beloved former pastor or esteemed layperson, may have run their course, but members may have a hard time letting go. Worship may have become stale or overly accommodating to individual tastes. The interim will have an eye for what may need to be pruned during an interim time to allow for new energy to emerge. However, none of this is done solo! An interim minister tests ideas with boards and committees, gets input and feedback, and listens carefully.

Continuing with agricultural metaphors, a garden is an extremely helpful one for understanding a congregation and the work done during the interim time. In their book *The Gardens of Democracy*, Eric Liu and Nick Hanauer distinguish between thinking of human community (a democracy is their concern) as a machine and as a garden. In a mechanistic world view, reality functions like a machine with numerous, replaceable parts. When a machine breaks down, you fix it. A living, organic entity such as a garden can't be "fixed" in the same way. It requires consistent cultivation, weeding, fertilizing, and watering. The authors describe how to move into this way of thinking, which they call "gardenbrain":

> Gardenbrain presupposes instability and unpredictability, and thus expects a continuous need for seeding, feeding, and weeding, ever-changing systems. To be a gardener is not to let nature take its course; it is to tend. It is to accept responsibility for nurturing the good growth and killing the bad.[4]

David Sawyer, director of Flourishing Congregations and retired professor of leadership and administration from Louisville Presbyterian Theological Seminary, applies this metaphor theologically. He reminds us that the word "tend" comes from the instruction that God gave to Adam to "till [tend the garden] and to keep it." Recent scholarship has demonstrated that a better translation of "to have dominion" over the creation is instead "to protect and defend" the good earth as stewards. This understanding helps us see God as a gardener who cultivates and tends to all of human activity as God does all of creation. Sawyer writes,

> Instead of a controlling, micromanager of a machinelike universe, God is pictured as a thoughtful collaborator with the realities of creation, ordering and nurturing the earth; patiently allowing for the work of the soil and seasons to come to fruition while guarding the long-term sustainability of the whole; encouraging the good and discouraging the destructive elements.[5]

Even though people may object, "But we like the ways things are," the metaphor of the church as a garden and the image of God as a horticulturist can help churches to see that there are no quick fixes or linear solutions. Rather, congregational life is interconnected, requiring intentional, tender care. As we work in harmony with the gardener, the garden, and the laws of horticulture, we create a diverse, fruitful plot of land. This image can balance the ecosystem of all of church life—education, spiritual growth, quality worship, caring fellowship, and service to the community—with a concern for long-term sustainability. The image of the church as a garden embraces the authentic identity and core values of the congregation instead of imposing remedies that might not actually fit.

When leaders embrace the image of the church as a garden, Sawyer asserts, they begin to see how all in the congregation is a web. In so doing, congregations may see that whatever is the presenting issue might not be the actual issue. Patterns and behaviors may become visible as we understand how a whole host of connections impact our life together. We don't live in isolation. What may seem to be a spat between the finance committee and allocating funds for the Sunday school could be about the wife of the chair of the finance committee being let go as the superintendent of the Sunday school program. Unclear boundaries, ambiguous organizational structures, and intense reactivity to relatively insignificant issues can be seen more clearly once we begin to see the ecology of the congregation.

I hope these metaphors are helpful in understanding that an interim minister is not there to shake things up, per se, but to help a congregation discover its own ecology, to pull some weeds to make room for growth, fertilize and water areas that have been neglected, and help churches reap a bumper crop. As I like to say, "I don't have a dog in this fight." In other words, it's not my church, and ultimately the congregation will do as it wishes. The interim, however, can be like the real estate agent who comes into your home and does what is called "staging." She assesses what needs improvement, furniture placement, curb appeal, and more to make your home appealing. These are things you cannot see because it's been home to you for many years.

Yet the time of transition is not "a holding pattern," a period of treading water until a "real minister" arrives. It's an important time to evaluate your past, assess the health of your present congregation, and prepare for the future. Do not waste the opportunity! The interim minister holds up a mirror to the congregation so they can see what she sees.

To use another analogy, the interim minister has a "balcony view" of the congregation.[6] Imagine what folks see on Sunday morning when they sit in the balcony. They see who arrives late. Who comes in with their children in tow. Who goes to the same pew they've sat in for forty years. Who's ushering this morning. But you also notice who's missing. Who's sitting alone. Who looks distressed. That the pastor snuck out through the side door to the parlor during the anthem and came back with his sermon.

In the same way, the interim pastor has the balcony or bird's eye view and sees things as an onlooker; he sees what others who are immersed in the congregation don't or won't see. For instance, an interim minister could ask folks in charge of worship and coffee hour afterward, "Did you notice that after visitors receive a bulletin from an usher they often stand around uncomfortably looking for a seat? Did you notice that they are often by themselves during coffee hour and no one engages them?" About administration, an interim minister might ask, "I've noticed that in order to reserve a room or schedule an event there are at least three forms to fill out. What is the history behind that? It seems a bit cumbersome for a church this size." Or regarding personal interactions she might ask, "I've observed that during meetings if a difficult subject comes up, someone always changes the subject. I'm wondering if this congregation is conflict averse and, if so, what's behind it?"

The interim minister may also make positive, affirming observations on the ground about matters of which the congregation was never aware. "I am so impressed by the number of mission projects this congregation is involved in! Tell me how that happened?" "You do such a good job caring for your seniors and homebound folks. How might you expand that ministry so others benefit as well?"

In this way, the interim minister shares an observation and asks the congregation or leadership "wondering questions" so they can chew on them and agree, disagree, or gain some insight.

I have a clergy colleague who over twenty-five years turned a small, aging, dying church around to a thriving, multicultural, missional congregation. He did so by asking folks to go back to the basics of the faith. "Why does the church exist and what is it called to do?" To hark back to the opening of this chapter, someone had moved their cheese and they needed to find new cheese. He told me, "Business as usual, even done well, no longer works." Because many churches "like the way things are," they will appeal to perhaps 10 to 20 percent of the U.S. population. By doing the hard but necessary work during a time of transition, congregations get their own view from the balcony to see who they are and what they need to do. They may see where the new cheese is.

We certainly don't have to mimic megachurches to be successful. God calls churches, just like human beings, to be uniquely themselves, using their gifts and doing what they do best. Of course, we like things the way they are. Patterns and customs give us comfort and security. But congregations can fall into ruts and boredom without examining those routines. Tailormade plans for your setting with a trained interim minister can help a congregation discover their best selves and capture renewed energy.

QUESTIONS FOR REFLECTION AND DISCUSSION

1. How does your congregation deal with stress during transition or change?
2. What are your church's best practices that you would like to bring forward? What do those practices reveal about what your congregation values?
3. What programs or practices do you think people are ready to let go of? Which of them are no longer working?
4. Consider inviting a person who has never attended your church to do so some Sunday morning. An unchurched person would be even better! Ask them to take notes and observe the service and fellowship hour afterward. Then interview them. What did they notice? How were they greeted? Did they understand the bulletin and the order of the service? What was the appearance of the building and grounds like? Afterward, gather leaders in the church and interview the "secret shopper." Find out what he observed and experienced. What surprised you? What can you do differently to improve things?

7

SHEPHERD, COACH, CONSULTANT, OR CHEERLEADER?

If you search the internet for the word "leader," you will get more than 300 million hits. There are 480,881 books on Amazon.com whose topics have to do with leaders. *Wikipedia* isn't much help either. Right off the bat, eleven distinct types of leaders are listed, from bureaucratic to transformational, to laissez-faire. Clearly there is a plethora of theories about leadership.

The leadership style that transitional leaders engage in is best called "transformational leadership." The goal of the interim pastor and the leadership team is to transform congregational culture to be as healthy, faithful, and effective as it can be. A leader who creates an inspiring vision of the future, motivates and inspires people to engage with that vision, and manages the delivery of the vision, is a leader people will follow. Robert Townsend once said, "A leader is a person with a magnet in his heart and a compass in his head."[1] The magnet draws people in, genuinely cares for them, listens to them, and motivates them to use their God-given gifts. The compass is the guiding vision, core values, and direction the pastoral leader feels called by God to pursue.

In the case of the interim leader, she will work closely with the transition team or other leadership circles to discern how to make best use of the time together, set goals, evaluate progress regularly, and imagine what the church will look like at the end of the time together. In ministry, there are no lone rangers. All are gifted members of the body of Christ and the work is impossible to do alone (1 Corinthians

12:27). Moreover, unless this work is empowered by the Holy Spirit and immersed in prayer, it will be no different than that of any corporation (John 15:7; Philippians 4:13).

SHEPHERD

An interim minister is a shepherd to the flock of God's people. In 1998, the late Roger S. Nicholson, a United Church of Christ pastor and leader in the development of interim ministry, edited a book called *Temporary Shepherds: A Congregational Handbook for Interim Ministry.*[2] The title is apt because while an interim minister will do much the same work as a settled pastor, he or she is temporary. A ritual I use on my first day leading worship in a new interim setting is to bring a walking stick to the pulpit with me. I explain that this is my shepherd's crook. I bring it with me and will keep it there while I am the shepherd of this flock—caring for its people, praying with them, teaching them, listening to them, counseling them, providing leadership and guidance for them.

I also receive keys from the board chair, moderator, warden, or another representative leader of the church. The keys are a symbol of the mutual ministry and trust we will share together. I remind the folks that one day I will take up my shepherd's crook, give back the keys, and leave this congregation because I am only a temporary shepherd. While we will share tears and laughter, joys and sorrows, accomplishments and disappointments, I will move on. I will no longer be their pastor nor they my flock. They will have a new spiritual leader once they call their new pastor.

To be effective, an interim minister must immerse himself in the lives of people in the congregation. It is difficult to preach to the needs and anxieties of people in the pews if the pastor is not mixing it up with the folk to know their struggles and their stories. That is what it means to be a shepherd under the Great Shepherd of the Sheep (John 10:1–18).

In addition to being a temporary shepherd, there are three other roles an interim specialist can play depending upon the circumstances of the church and presenting issues. The interim can function as a coach, a consultant, a cheerleader—or all three!

COACH

Coaching is quickly becoming one of the leading tools and strategies that people and organizations are using to enhance their effectiveness. By asking penetrating questions and offering insightful feedback, a coach helps those being coached to discover their latent strengths and inner resources. The coach then helps them to discover what they want to accomplish professionally and personally in their life and establish goals to meet those desires. The coach also holds the coachees accountable to meet those goals between meetings.

A coach asks the individual or the group powerful questions that prompt them to think more deeply and get out of mental ruts that bog them down. Coaches promote creativity and exploring inner resources that have been dormant or underutilized.

Asking good questions, or "wondering questions," as I call them, prompts thinking about the purpose and goals of a program or practice and, ideally, puts the work back on the group. For instance, a church I served was thinking about having a contemporary service in addition to the traditional one. I could have given my opinion and said the timing was wrong during a transitional period, "You don't have the resources," "The congregation isn't asking for it," and so on. Instead, I asked a series of questions.

- What would the purpose be?
- Why now?
- Is there a demand/need for such a service? Is the assumption that "if we build it they will come," or is the need actually arising from the congregation?
- Do we have the resources?
- What kind of service would it be?
- Is the assumption that because nondenominational evangelical churches attract people that way, it will therefore work here? Will that model translate well to our church, which is a different culture with different needs, wants, and theology?
- Should a new project of this magnitude be started during a transitional time when the current pastor will be leaving and the new pastor may not want to do this?

- Should this idea be part of a wider vision asking the congregation for their input?
- Would a "blended" service be more appropriate, using both contemporary and traditional music and worship elements? What resources might be put toward that?

These questions led to a profitable and lively discussion about worship, music, generational differences, the process for making decisions, and how the vision of the church should drive new ministries.

Lovett H. Weems Jr., the director of the Lewis Center for Church Leadership, says "Leaders do not need answers. Leaders must have the right questions."[3] When questioning becomes a way of life for a leader, a vast constituency of free "counselors" (the congregation) offers clues, ideas, patterns, and discoveries that the pastoral leader would not otherwise know.

In seeking to understand the identity of your congregation, Weems offers these examples of effective questions from Nancy T. Ammerman and Carl S. Dudley as being useful:[4]

- If someone asked you about our church, what story would you tell them?
- If you could tell a new resident only one thing about our church, what would it be?

One congregation used the following questions when they observed that participation and energy levels varied considerably among their programs:

- What programs thrive without extraordinary promotion and encouragement?
- What programs struggle no matter what we do?
- What can we learn from the first group as we begin new programs?

Evaluation is an excellent way to make good things better. Weems suggests three simple questions to use after any undertaking:

- What did we do right?
- What did we do wrong?

- What else should we have done?

Weems also recommends these questions written by David Roozen, a sociologist who studies congregational life and planning:

- Who are we? (mission and values)
- Where are we? (assessment)
- Where are we going? (vision and priorities)
- How are we going to get there? (planning and goals)
- When will it be done? (scheduling)
- Who is responsible for what? (delegating)
- How much will it cost? (budgeting)
- Did we do it? (evaluation)[5]

The goal of coaching is not to fix things, but to help individuals and institutions discover their own solutions with the help of the interim minister. She can offer recommendations and resources that have worked for her and see if leaders want to try some. Coaching is a tool that can help a person or church reach Jesus's desire for us: "I came that they might have life and have it abundantly" (John 10: 10).

CONSULTANT

Consultants, on the other hand, are hired more often to recommend a strategy to resolve a problem or to identify ways to be a better organization. A church may hire a consultant or work with a staff member of the denomination who has expertise in stewardship, church growth, governance, best practices for finance committees, and more. This is an especially good time to tend to an issue that has been put off or neglected for too long.

An interim minister can use his or her experience and expertise to tackle a problem or improve a process. It could be to redo the annual stewardship program, create a policy and procedures manual, update job descriptions for staff or boards and committees, or address a long-running conflict that simmers just below the surface of the congregation.

I, for instance, led three different congregations to rethink and rewrite their bylaws at their behest. Their structures had become too cumbersome and no longer supported their ministries. Many positions on boards and committees went unfilled because the culture had changed. There were fewer stay-at-home moms, retirees often travelled two to three months a year, and young adults did not find committee work particularly meaningful. People wanted a structure that was more streamlined that gave people freedom to meet and work with more flexibility. The end would be to promote the vision, not just to support the institution. At one congregation, we used a workbook called *Flexible, Missional Constitution/Bylaws.* [6] The working group read the manual, met regularly, and designed a model of ministry teams. There was a vision team that regularly reviewed if the church was on task; a Christian formation team that was responsible for Sunday school, adult education, youth groups, and small groups; a resource team that handled buildings and grounds, finances, and stewardship; a worship team that oversaw music, worship, and drama at all worship settings; and a mission and outreach team that kept in touch with ministries the church supported, organized hands-on projects, and fostered church growth and vitality. The teams were not to do the work themselves but were created to recruit volunteers for specific projects based upon volunteers' interests and skills. Sections of the existing bylaws were suspended for a year while the congregation lived into the new model. It would be evaluated and adjusted at the next congregational meeting.

What's the Difference?

In many ways coaches and consultants require the same skills: they both need to know how to ask good questions, listen well, share feedback, and promote positive actions. Coaches differ in that they lead others toward their own conclusions and actions. A coach who is working with a university president does not presume to know how to run a university. Instead, the coach helps the president discover ideas about fundraising, attracting quality faculty, or building programs in science and technology, for example, and move him or her into action. Coaching in its purest form is content free. However, some coaching models are hybrids of coaching and consulting.

Coaches ask more than they tell. Good consultants also ask a lot of questions, but they usually are gathering information to offer a solution. Both coaches and consultants ask good questions that reflect interest in the client and offer feedback about what they see and hear. You're more likely to open up to someone who is curious about you.

A consultant's expertise is the main thing they have to share with you. Coaches have expertise too, but they usually share it when you ask for their help or they first ask permission to offer advice. Expertise in a certain area is sometimes the thing that is most needed. Coaches and consultants both find out what's really going on and what the congregation really wants. Then they can share expertise in a personalized and targeted manner, providing what the client needs at the appropriate time.

Consultants often conduct interviews, look at data, and make assessments. They then have information to share and specific recommendations to make about what needs to be done. A coach may offer assessments, but they are often shared as observations to be pondered, rather than plans to be followed.

Sometimes what is needed is hard data and a plan of action. That's when an interim minister will act as a consultant. Other times a church needs to get clear about where they really want to go and what they really value. If that's the case, the congregation is better off with the interim minister as a coach. Regardless, both coaching and consulting is about growth, creativity, and transformation! The truth is, most consultants do a little coaching and most coaches do some consulting.[7]

CHEERLEADER

A transitional minister is also a cheerleader. He encourages the congregation, shares what he thinks their strengths are, points out things they do well, and praises them for work well done. An interim minister helps congregations look beyond the four walls of the sanctuary by reminding them who they are (the body of Christ) and what they are called to do and be (build a portion of God's kingdom in their corner of the world). A cheerleader is not a Pollyanna who sees the world through rose-colored glasses, but someone who is able to look wide-eyed at a congregation with all its warts and wrinkles yet see its beauty marks as well. We try to look at our settings through the "spectacles of scripture," as John Calvin put it.

An interim leader will use preaching, worship, and other settings to remind the congregation of the great biblical stories of God's faithfulness through times of exile, challenge, and anxiety. In Acts 4:36, Barnabas was called a "Son of Encouragement." What a great name to be given—someone who has a reputation for inspiring those around him to keep pressing on, to keep trusting God.

Leaders can encourage a congregation with stories like God calling Abraham and Sarah to leave their retirement home and go to a land yet unknown. Or God calling Moses to lead the Israelites out of Egypt into a promised land. Or Nehemiah encouraging the exiles returning from Babylon to Jerusalem as they rebuilt the walls of the city. Or like Daniel when he walked into the lions' den and the red-hot furnace yet experienced God's salvation. Or the disciples and the Apostle Paul who built the early church against all odds. These are just a few of the many stories in the Bible that intersect with our story as we walk through an in-between time.

There are also practical ways an interim pastor can encourage a church (and teach their leaders to do the same), particularly if they are feeling poorly about themselves, small or insignificant. Here's my top-ten list.

1. Tell people that you believe in them and that they can do the hard but necessary work. Lift up successes from the past and encourage people to do more of the same. Focus on the positive.
2. Offer people words of praise and be specific. "You did a great job at . . ."; "I really appreciate that you . . ."; "I was really impressed that you . . ." Describe their value. "You're the best [fill in the blank] we have."
3. Remember the power of presence. Make eye contact. Use good listening skills. Give your full attention. Smile. Validate their feelings. Never discount or say, "You shouldn't feel that way." That is depreciating, not encouraging.
4. Send cards and notes letting people know that you're thinking about them and praying for them.
5. When you see someone making positive changes in their lives, affirm them. "You seem to have a really great attitude about . . ."; "It may be that I'm just starting to take notice, but I see that you're . . ."; "Do you think that you are becoming more . . . ?"

6. Tell people how they've encouraged you!

7. When someone is discouraged or hurting, offer specific, practical help. If you ask, "How can I help?" the person might be at a loss to answer. It's better to ask, "Would it help if I . . . ?" or say, "I would like to . . ."

8. Celebrate key accomplishments, life passages, and have fun! Churches can become so serious during a transitional time that they forget how a good laugh or a fun experience can be a boost to morale.

9. Remember the power of touch. When appropriate, an affirming pat on the back, a squeeze of the elbow, or a hug goes a long way. In a high-tech world, we can't forget how meaningful a touch can be.

10. Above all, remind people regularly that God loves them with an everlasting love. There's nothing they can do to make God love them more and there's nothing they can do to make God love them less.

OTHER JOBS TO BE DONE

Terry Foland, former board member of the Interim Ministry Network and consultant for the Alban Institute, suggests these as tasks that congregations may address in addition to the focus points of the transitional period.[8]

- **Rebuild the Congregational "Infrastructure."** This rebuilding is what we did in the example I just gave. It is a thorough review of the administrative structures, processes and procedures, and practical efficiency.

- **Evaluate and Remove Staff Members If Necessary:** Congregations usually don't have a systematic process in place to evaluate staff members on a regular basis, particularly if everything is going well. Annual mutual ministry reviews in which the ministry and not just the staff member is evaluated is much more helpful and less threatening. The focus is on the ministry of the entire church and not just the staff member. The most difficult staff problems usually arise when an employee is also a church member. She can become entrenched, does not keep clear boundaries between her role as a church staff person and as a church member, or no longer has the skills to do the job well. If a person is fired or receives a poor evaluation, his friends may rally to his defense, causing a major brouhaha. The congregation is more willing to deal with a difficult employee with the interim minister's leadership than to postpone it until a new pastor is in place. This is because the interim pastor will be leaving and will not have to live with the fallout of having let someone go in the way a settled pastor would. Plus, the new pastor will not have to deal with the "hassle" of a recalcitrant staff member early in her tenure.

- **Address Financial and Stewardship Issues.** Stewardship does not necessarily have to drop or go flat during a transitional period. Giving may be down when a pastor leaves, especially if he left under a cloud or coasted to her retirement. Ongoing education about the spiritual benefits of faithful giving and trying fresh efforts and new methods can inspire greater commitment and boost financial support under interim ministerial leadership.

- **Resolve Conflicts over Issues, Agendas, or Priorities.** Latent issues that have been buried, ignored, or denied often emerge during an interim period. An interim minister who has no skin in the game can often be more objective because he or she doesn't know the players or the history, and has less of a vested interest in the outcome than a settled pastor. Because she is trained in conflict management, she will be better able to facilitate the conversation and help parties to come to some kind of resolution. An important goal during the interim time is to resolve such conflict before a new pastor is called.

- **Mediate Interpersonal or Intergroup Conflicts.** If a conflict has been simmering or emerges during the transitional period, an interim pastor will probably be able to serve as an objective third party mediator. He or she will not be worried about long-term relationships with the individuals or groups involved in the skirmish. Consequently, the interim pastor can be more direct in naming the issues and dynamics of the interactions. Hopefully, the principals involved can more readily focus on the issues at hand and their resolution rather than wonder whether the pastor is on my side or theirs.

- **Get Closure with the Previous Pastor.** Every parting of a settled or interim minister should have a ceremony of farewell and closure. Most liturgies developed for this purpose include a statement about how the minister will no longer be the church's pastor and the congregation will no longer look to the pastor for care and support. An interim pastor can educate a congregation about the importance of honoring the end of a relationship to make way for new clergy leadership. Weaning the previous pastor from the church can be another matter. If the previous pastor or church members cross boundaries, this behavior can impede the work of the interim pastor and the arriving pastor and the judicatory should be notified.
- **Improve Communication.** As a settled pastor begins to look for a new call, some things may have become neglected. Regular communication with the congregation is often one of them. Almost every congregation I've served has said "Improving communication" is one of the goals of the interim period. This a prime time to enhance communication processes through bulletins, newsletters, email blasts, "church chats" on a quarterly basis, or whatever best suits the congregation.

In addition, Foland has compiled a set of questions from every arena of congregational life to explore during the interim time.[9] Found in the appendix G, these are questions leaders or members of the transition team can ponder before the interim minister arrives and throughout the process.

Whether as a coach, consultant, cheerleader, or shepherd, an interim minister worth his or her salt will inspire confidence as the spiritual leader of the church. This confidence can come from four sources during the interim time: the interim carries out his ministry well; the congregation is experiencing increasing health and strength; small successes are happening regularly; the congregation recaptures a positive self-esteem about who they are; and, most important, the congregation finds a renewed trust in the faithfulness of God.

I had a seminary professor who said after he walked out of worship at Westminster Chapel in London under the preaching of G. Campbell Morgan, "I felt like I was ten feet tall." "It wasn't because he told us how great we were, but he told us how great our God was." We aren't carried and upheld during wilderness times because we have a wonderful faith in God. It's because we have faith in a wonderful God.

QUESTIONS FOR REFLECTION AND DISCUSSION

1. Look at appendix H, "Self-Image Assessment for Local Churches." Have each person in your group follow the instructions and then reflect upon the images you chose. How will these images impact what kind of minister you should hire?
2. What style of leadership does your congregation best respond to? What style do you think is needed during this time of transition?
3. Where do you think the church needs a Shepherd? Coach? Consultant? Cheerleader?

8

LIKE A SHARK: MOVE FORWARD OR DIE

Certain sharks, such as the great white, mako, and whale sharks, must constantly swim to keep oxygen-rich ocean water flowing over their gills. If they stop moving, they will die from lack of oxygen. These sharks have lost the ability and the necessary anatomy to move water over their gills using their mouth muscles. Instead, they can only respire by ramming ocean water over their gills as they swim forward.

Churches can be like this. They settle into a way of doing and being and have stopped moving forward or their anatomy (structures, ministries, programs) no longer work as they once did. Therefore, they must keep moving forward or they will die.

This may sound a bit melodramatic, especially if you are a church that is thriving or holding your own, but to remain vital, churches must always be moving forward by reassessing their purpose, mission, vision, and goals. In this chapter I will introduce you to ideas, strategies, and models that will help congregations assess their vitality and move forward during a transitional time.

TRADITION, CONVENTION, AND RETRADITIONING

Churches value tradition perhaps more than most human organizations. Those traditions are important because they carry sacred meaning and memory. Traditions can become an anchor that holds congregations in place or a launching pad that can propel them into a new future. There is a difference between tradition and traditionalism, which is helpful for congregations to understand. Tradition usually means something that is deeply rooted in the Christian faith that springs from scripture, Christian teachings, and practices. These would be things like Bible study, prayer, the sacraments, worship, and service. Tradition with a capital *T* is the big picture, if you will, of the historic Christian faith. Traditionalism, with a small *t*, is the practices and habits followed in individual churches and communities.

Church historian Jaroslov Pelikan puts it succinctly: "Tradition is the living faith of the dead; traditionalism is the dead faith of the living. Tradition lives in conversation with the past, while remembering where we are and when we are and that it is we who have to decide."[1]

Tradition is that churches observe four Sundays of Advent before Christmas and read the birth story from Luke on Christmas Eve. Traditionalism is that the Snowflake Fair must always be the second Saturday during Advent. Tradition is that the sacrament of baptism is a rite of initiation into the Christian church. Traditionalism is that the newly baptized always receive a candle and a prayer shawl, and the congregation has cake during coffee hour. This is not to discount local traditions but to make sure we do not confuse them with the larger Tradition of the Christian story.

There is also confusion between tradition and convention. Conventions are often mistaken for traditions. As a historian and observer of American church life, Diana Butler Bass shares a poignant story in her book *The Practicing Congregation: Imaging a New Old Church*.[2] She tells of the time when she wanted to host an Advent study group at her local church and teach methods of praying with the birth stories. She couldn't find a meeting space because all the rooms were taken up by preparations for the Christmas fair. She went round and round and head to head with the chair of the Christmas fair committee to work something out. Finally, the chair said in a huff, "The problem with you is that you don't appreciate tradition!" Butler Bass was aghast. She was a professional historian. If anyone knew about tradition, it was she. The disgruntled chair was confusing the convention of the local church with the great tradition of the Christian church.

I share this to demonstrate the dynamics that can occur in a congregation, particularly during a transition. Churches can unreflexively hold on to local traditions to keep a sense of equilibrium and serenity during the interim time. Yet what some see as familiar and comfortable may be a rut for others. This might be a time to consider that what you thought were traditions are actually conventions that are up for review.

In spite of an indifference toward tradition in secular culture, Butler Bass contends that people are still hungry for tradition, ritual, and symbols that help make meaning out of life. She encourages congregations to engage in *fluid retraditioning*. This approach asks that congregations recognize the changes going on around them and find ways to work creatively with those shifts. These congregations are willing to "change the package," she says, by innovating their forms and practices to introduce or reintroduce the tradition in a new package. In other words, take appropriate ancient Christian traditions and practices and reappropriate them for twenty-first-century people.

CHURCH LIFE CYCLES

Another tool to help congregations understand whether they are moving forward, drifting, or drowning is to look at their life cycle. Just as human beings and ecosystems have life cycles, so do churches. The life cycle of a salmon, for instance, moves from egg, to adult, to spawner, to death. If left unchecked, there is a tendency for every local church to progress through a life cycle, from birth through growth, through middle and old age, and ultimately to death.

George W. Bullard Jr., of the Columbia Leadership Group, graphs the life cycle of a congregation into ten distinct phases (see table 8.1, next page). He envisions the life cycle as a bell curve with five steps on the upside and five on the downside.[3]

Bullard also observes that there are four organizing principles in every church, some of which are more dominant than others during each phase of the life cycle: vision, relationships, program, and management.

- **Vision** is the spiritual and strategic direction of a local congregation, cast by the leadership and owned by the membership.
- **Relationships** bring people to faith, help them assimilate into the life and ministry of the congregations, and provide opportunities for spiritual growth, building supportive relationships and service.

Table 8.1.

UPSIDE OF LIFE CYCLE	DOWNSIDE OF LIFE CYCLE
Birth	Maturity
Infancy	Empty Nest
Childhood	Retirement
Adolescence	Old Age
Adulthood	Death

- **Programs** are the activities that support relationships: worship services, educational opportunities, community building, ministries of service, and connections to ecumenical, interfaith, and community organizations.
- **Management** is the administration of resources, programs, buildings and grounds, and the governing structures that support the programs and relationships.

Bullard uses a car to illustrate how these principles apply to a local church. Vision drives. Relationships sit next to Vision to navigate. Program sits behind Relationships, and Management sits behind Vision. When the church is newly planted or very young, the vision and relationships drive the car. Then as the church grows, it needs programs and management to drive the vision and build relationships. When a church is at its prime, all four components are of equal importance and in their appropriate seats. They are running on all four cylinders.

Bullard observes that when a church gets tired, it can become complacent and fall into a maintenance mode. The vision flags or is forgotten. At that point management tends to climb into the driver's seat and the church's goal becomes maintenance or survival. The longer management drives, the more passive a congregation becomes.

Decline and death are not inevitable. This model is not a predictor of what will happen, but what might happen if leaders do not pay attention to a creeping loss of vision. Understanding church life cycles is key to helping leaders assess their position on the bell curve and take steps during the interim time to address what they learn.

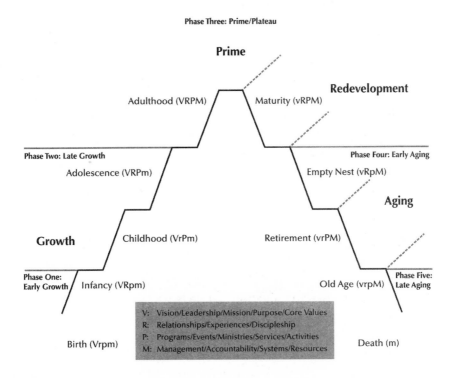

Figure 8.1.   Copyright 2000, Rev. George Bullard, D. Min.

RENEWAL, REVITALIZATION, OR REDEVELOPMENT

Many of our old-line, mainline, historic churches are a shadow of their former selves for many of the reasons we discussed in chapter 1, "It's Not Your Parents' Church Anymore." They are looking for programs and practices to get their vitality back. This is another way of moving forward like the shark. A lot of "re" words float around church revival programs—revitalize, renew, reenvision, reinvent, redevelop, restart, replant, and resurrect. Looking at ways to revitalize a church follows naturally from our discussion of church life cycles, especially if they are on the downward side of the bell curve. The way to restore vitality is not by attempting to climb back up the right side of the downward slope, trying to reach the "good old days." Rather, new approaches must be made to restore vision and relationships. An interim minister can help them find new energy by introducing renewal practices. Many denominations are initiating programs to help congregations become vital. It might mean having a consultant do a thorough review of your property, finances, and programs and help you discover a bold new vision based upon your assets and energy. It could mean joining a cluster of churches who are trained and coached by a specialist in restoring church vitality. Or, in a worst-case scenario, it might mean deciding that it's time to close and leave a legacy of your assets to the next generation.

In their book *Redeveloping the Congregation: A How-to for Lasting Change*, Mary Sellon, Dan Smith, and Gail Grossman, pastors together at an American Baptist church, offer descriptions of three of the most common ways of thinking about enhancing congregational vitality and reversing a downward trend in a church's life cycle: renewal, revitalization, and redevelopment.[4]

- **Renewal** is pursued when a congregation realizes that it has become inward focused and needs to begin moving outside of the four walls of the church. Perhaps they feel that they are just going through the motions and things have become flat and stale. So the focus turns to understanding the hopes and the hurts of their surrounding community and creating ministries that meet those needs. Congregations in renewal pay attention to every aspect of church life: energizing worship, strengthening caregiving and community building, and helping people grow spiritually with intentionality. Renewal also means bathing everything in prayer, studying scripture, and meeting in small support groups. In John 7:37–38 Jesus gave this invitation: "Let anyone who is thirsty come to me, and let the one who believes in me drink. As the scripture has said, 'Out of the believer's heart shall flow rivers of living water.'" The work of renewal cannot be done without filling our spiritual wells. We cannot give away what we don't have.
- **Revitalization** is required when most of the energy of a church is focused on maintenance and preservation. This process requires more time and energy than renewal does. The hard work of learning again what the New Testament teaches about the purpose and ministry of the church, then discerning the purpose of *your* church and God's unique call for you are important parts of this process.
- **Redevelopment** is needed when the congregation's energy flows almost exclusively toward its own survival. When the faith com-

munity becomes a gated community rather than a living body that transforms lives and serve others, death is inevitable. Turning around a church in this situation is the most difficult of the three.

While there may not be time, given the constraints of the interim period, to implement any of the approaches above, the interim could be used to discern and explore if such a program should be started with a new settled pastor.

TECHNICAL VERSUS ADAPTIVE PROBLEMS

The kinds of challenges churches face these days requires reframing how we look at the problems before us. Ron Heifetz, leadership guru at Harvard business school, makes the observation that all human organizations, including churches, have to adapt or die (like the shark).[5] We witness the same pattern in the biological world: when the environment changes, species need to learn to adapt or they go extinct. Most institutions, Heifetz observes, are used to solving technical problems, that is, when they see a problem, they brainstorm about familiar solutions and apply them to the problem. So, for instance, if you have a sinus infection, you go to your doctor, she asks your symptoms and prescribes an antibiotic, and within a week to ten days the infection is gone.

An adaptive problem is one that requires us to change our values, attitudes, or habits of behavior to arrive at a solution.[6] When you have a rare form of cancer for which there is no known cure, you try different treatments and protocols, which are often trial and error. You might combine that with homeopathic therapy, diet, exercise, and meditation. You are kind of making it up as you go along. These are the type of problems many congregations face.

For a local church, a technical problem is, "Where do we find another room for our sixth grade Sunday school class?" An adaptive problem is, "Given the competition we have with athletics, the crazy schedules of families, and the cyberworld, what might a ministry that reaches middle school students look like?"

A technical problem might be, "What kind of advertising can we do to get more people to come to worship?" An adaptive problem is, "Given that there isn't any social pressure to go to church and traditional churches don't attract people like they once did, what are some ministries we might try to get people to come in through the side doors instead of the front doors?"

A technical problem is, "What can we do to get more people to step up and fill the empty slots on boards and committees?" An adaptive problem might be, "Given that people don't have the time or inclination to be on committees, how we might redesign the structure of our church to accommodate the schedules and interests of our people and better support our ministries? How can we help them discover their spiritual gifts and find places for them to use them? How might we make them spiritual support groups as well as task teams?" An adaptive approach to problems helps congregations to be flexible and creative, and move through change that enables them to thrive.[7]

Whereas technical change requires us to do things differently, adaptive change requires us to think differently about what we're doing and so, as Heifetz writes, requires a change in values and beliefs as well as behaviors. The chart in table 8.2 lays out the differences clearly.[8]

An example of the difference between a technical and an adaptive solution to a problem is taking medication to lower blood pressure versus changing your lifestyle by eating healthy, getting more exercise, and lowering stress. A technical solution to lowering the incidents of drunk driving would be to increase the penalty for driving while intoxi-

Table 8.2.

TECHNICAL PROBLEMS	ADAPTIVE CHALLENGES
Easy to identify.	Difficult to identify (easy to deny).
Often lend themselves to quick and easy solutions.	Require changes in values, beliefs, roles, relationships, and approaches to work.
Often can be solved by the authority of an expert.	People with the problem do the work of solving it.
Require change in just one or a few places; often contained within organizational boundaries.	Require change in numerous places; usually cross organizational boundaries.
People are generally receptive to technical solutions.	People often resist even acknowledging adaptive challenges.
Solutions can often be implemented quickly—even by edict.	Solutions require experiments and new discoveries; they can take a long time to implement and cannot be implemented by edict.

cated. An adaptive solution would be to raise public awareness of the danger and effects of drunk driving, targeting teenagers in particular.

A wonderful illustration about a technical solution versus an adaptive change is found in the movie *Moneyball* based on the book of the same title by Michael Lewis.[9] Billy Beane, the irascible manager, is gathered with his scouts. The scouts are old school and believe the problem of having losing, uncompetitive teams is that they've got less money to work with and have to contend with richer teams. Their solution is to continue scouting, trust their gut instincts, and thereby find better recruits and develop them into exceptional players. Billy argues that television has fundamentally changed the game, so he advocates not just doing things better, but understanding the game entirely differently by looking at data often overlooked. Through the use of what is called cybermetrics, computer-based sports analytics, he determined, among many other things, that teams who had players with a higher on-base percentage scored more runs. He consequently hired players that fit that bill and turned the team around without well-known, high-paid ballplayers.

The technical solution was to have old school scouts size up young recruits, trust their instincts, and develop young players into superlative players. The adaptive solution was to use computer-generated data on often overlooked statistics to see correlations between those numbers and successful ball players.

The stewardship committee conducts the annual stewardship campaign as it has for the last five years even though pledges have been dropping. That is a technical solution to try to raise funds. An adaptive solution would be to have people interview one another during worship about what they love about their church and share what they heard from one another. Ask what would be missing if the church no longer existed. They would then be asked to pledge to support a church that they love and would leave a huge hole in their hearts and the community if the church was gone.

AN APPRECIATIVE APPROACH

Churches that are stalled or drifting have often lost a positive focus, whether it's about the Gospel's ability to change lives or the good they are or could be doing. Too many of our churches are so "problem saturated" that they can't see all of the gifts, assets, and positives of their life together. They focus on their deficits—we're a small church, we don't have much money, we don't have any young families, or we always seem to be fighting about something.

What is needed is a fresh look at what the church values, what is going well, what their assets are, and what a future dream might look like. The congregations need to appreciate who they are and what they do well. Appreciative inquiry, as it is called, is a method and a practice used by many corporations, nonprofits, community organizations, and churches to mine resources and possibilities that lie within the organization.

The following list highlights the premises of appreciative inquiry:

- In every organization, some things work well. (Find it out and do more of it!)
- What we focus on becomes reality. (If we focus on negatives that's all we see.)
- Asking questions influences the group. (Asking the right questions promotes creativity and shared responsibility.)
- People have more confidence in the journey to the future when they carry forward parts of the past. (Bringing a ritual, practice, program, or sacred object into the next chapter of their life assures folks that it won't be entirely different.)
- If we carry parts of the past into the future, they should be what is best about the past. (Signature moments in the life of the church of which they are proud.)
- It is important to value differences. (Homogeneity is boring. The body of Christ has many parts and many gifts.)
- The language we use creates our reality. ("Ain't it awful" is a downer. "Thank God for my life" lifts your chin.)
- Organizations are heliotropic. Just as sunflowers turn to the sun for light and energy, social systems and people evolve toward the most positive images they hold of themselves and this is true for churches. (Churches should turn toward Jesus Christ the light of the world.)
- Outcomes should be useful. (The result should be practical, measurable, and life giving.)

- All work together is collaborative. (The process is a collective effort based on the shared values of the group.)[10]

The appreciative inquiry process begins by congregants interviewing one another about what they value about themselves, their church, and their experiences within it. They are asked to tell stories about best experiences and how they might replicate those more often. All of these stories are then gathered to find common patterns and shared values. For an example of an interview, see appendix I.

The difference between the typical method of problem solving and appreciative inquiry can be profound. In problem solving the process begins with a "felt need," then moves through the following stages:

1. Identification of Problem
2. Analysis of Causes
3. Analysis of Possible Solutions
4. Action Plan / Treatment

This differs from the steps in an appreciative inquiry process:

1. Introduce leaders to theory and practice, deciding the focus and developing initial steps to discover the organization's "best."
2. Inquire about "the best" of the church's stories, practices, and dreams. This would be the interview process we looked at above.
3. Imagine "what might be" by imagining together and building toward consensus concerning "what should be."
4. Innovate "what will be" through discussion, commitment, and equipping, with the largest possible level of participation.

Using the appreciative inquiry process during a time of transition can help a congregation discover its core values, recover a sense of confidence about who they are, and imagine a future together that they can work toward.

GOD IS YOUR GRAVITY

The long and short of this chapter is not to discourage you, but to cheer you on! It's a word of encouragement to keep looking out the wind-

shield instead of the rearview mirror. A transitional time is an excellent
opportunity to take stock, reflect, and imagine an inspiring future toward which God is pulling you. God is your gravity! When the people of
Judah were exiled to Babylon they were distraught. All that had been
familiar, comfortable, and secure was gone. But Jeremiah told them,

> Build houses and live in them; plant gardens and eat what they pro-
> duce. Take wives and have sons and daughters; take wives for your
> sons, and give your daughters in marriage, that they may bear sons
> and daughters; multiply there, and do not decrease. But seek the
> welfare of the city where I have sent you into exile, and pray to the
> Lord on its behalf, for in its welfare you will find your welfare. (Jere-
> miah 29: 4–7)

In other words, he told them not to lament for the past, but to live in
the present. Bloom where you're planted. Create a future. God had not
abandoned them in their exile. They would be in Babylon for only
seventy years. And behind the mess and in spite of it was God. Then the
Lord gave these amazing words of encouragement, "For surely I know
the plans I have for you, says the Lord, plans for your welfare and not
for harm, to give you a future with hope. Then when you call upon me
and come and pray to me, I will hear you" (Jeremiah 29: 11).

Like Judah, churches that are between settled pastors may feel like
they are in exile. They may be tempted to look with nostalgia to the
past. But as God said to Israel, God also says to you, "Get to work. Do it
well. I have plans and a future for you."

QUESTIONS FOR REFLECTION AND DISCUSSION

1. How do you see the distinctions between tradition, traditionalism, convention, and retraditioning playing out in your church?
2. Where would you place your church on the life cycle curve?
   What are the dominant forces driving your church? Vision? Relationships? Program? Or Management? Using the car image, who
   is in the driver's seat, the passenger's seat, behind the driver, and
   behind the passenger? Should they change seats and, if so, how
   might you do this?

3. How do you respond to the three *R*s of renewal, revitalization, and redevelopment? Do any resonate with you about where your church is? Should your church engage in any of these processes?

4. How is the difference between a technical or adaptive solution to a problem helpful? Can you come up with some examples from your setting?

5. How would using an appreciative inquiry approach to problem solving and planning be helpful for your church? What intrigues you about it?

9

READY, SET, GO . . .

The work is almost done. The search committee has done its job and they are ready to present a candidate as your settled pastor to the congregation. Anticipation is in the air. You are eager and curious to meet this person who will be your pastor and spiritual leader for the unknown future.

To assure the success of the incoming pastor, good preparations are crucial. Working closely with your interim pastor and your denominational executives, there are practical matters to be completed before the new pastor arrives on the scene. Make sure preparations have been made and finalized in the following key areas.

CONTRACT OR COVENANT

Most denominations have a template for a contract or covenant. They may go under different titles such as A Letter of Call Agreement. In strictly legal terms, a contract is a voluntary agreement between two or more parties, who intend to create legal obligations, in which there is a promise to do or perform some work or service for a valuable consideration or benefit. It is enforceable by law. A covenant, on the other hand, is an agreement or written promise between two or more parties that constitutes a pledge to do or refrain from doing something.[1] Christian organizations would be well served to keep the nature of "covenant" in mind—to inform the legal document with certain scriptural principles.

Covenant is a biblical term that evokes the principles of mutuality, integrity, and partnership under God's gracious presence. Mutuality is the reality that the pastor and the church are in ministry together. The minister is not the "hired gun," to do all the spiritual stuff like praying and preaching and pastoral care. Nor is he or she the resident "Holy person" to be placed on a pedestal of impossible expectations. Together you are engaged in mutual ministry to build the reign of God in your corner of the world together. Consequently, there will be promises your pastor makes to you and promises you make to your pastor. The agreement is actually a three-way covenant because God witnesses these mutual promises. Nevertheless, there are practical matters that need to be negotiated.

Each denomination likely has its own model for a covenant or contract and you should be in touch with the judicatory official of your region to find that out. Nevertheless, there are components that are found in almost every template. They include items such as the following:

- **A Preamble.** This lays down the faith foundation of the call to ministry and the nature of the covenant between the pastor and the church. Each denomination will have its own language.
- **The Time of Work.** The hours or blocks of work per week that the church and pastor agree to. Typically, this is 45 to 50 hours per week or ten to twelve blocks per week, a block being defined as a morning, afternoon, or evening. Normally a pastor will work two blocks per day. You will also want to account for time away.

  - **Vacation and Days Off.** Vacations are usually four weeks per year including five Sundays. All national holidays are also days off.
  - **Parental Leave.** Parental leave is granted for the birth or adoption of a child. Twelve weeks is often the norm.
  - **Personal and Sick Days.** These usually accumulate one day per month, collecting twelve days a year as needed. Personal days for bereavement, family emergencies, and personal care are three to five days per incident, not to exceed ten to twelve days total per year.

- **Study Leave.** Study leave is usually two weeks per year including Sundays for continuing education, retreats, and renewal.

- **Compensation**

  - **Cash Salary.** Annual salary is determined using the guidelines of your denomination including factors such as years of experience, size of the church, level of education, and so forth.
  - **Housing or Housing Allowance.** If the compensation package includes a parsonage or manse, all utilities, maintenance, and expenses related to upkeep of the home are included. A housing allowance is usually based on the median value of houses in the community. The method for determining the exact amount is spelled out in the tax code. If a congregation has a total package in mind, salary and housing allowance amounts can be adjusted, depending on what the pastor is legally entitled to claim as housing.
  - **Social Security and Medicare Contributions.** The church will pay half of these.

- **Benefits**

  - **Pension.** Often the plan is carried by the denomination.
  - **Health Insurance.** A health plan could be covered by a denominational or commercial plan.
  - **Dental and Eye Care Insurance.** These may or may not be part of a health insurance plan and need to be purchased separately.
  - **Group Life and Disability Insurance.**
  - **Workers' Comprehensive Insurance.** In the event of an accident or injury while on church property or doing church-related business, you will need to include workers' insurance.

- **Expense Reimbursement**

  - **Mileage.** For church-related business at the current IRS reimbursement rate.
  - **Continuing Education Funds.**
  - **Office Support.** Office space, equipment, and a secretary or administrative assistant should be provided.
  - **Discretionary Fund.** For pastoral emergencies or benevolence for parishioners or those in need.

- **Other Agreements**

  - **Reasonable Moving Expenses.**
  - **Moving Date.**
  - **Start Date (and the day salary and benefits begin).**

- **Mutual Ministry Review.** An annual review not just of the pastor, but of the whole ministry involving the leadership of the church as well as staff. It should focus on mutually agreed-upon goals, assessment of the successes and disappointments, and renewed clarity of mutual expectations. If there is conflict or disagreement, a third party may be asked to conduct the review.
- **Sabbatical.** After at least five but no more than seven years, a three- to six-month sabbatical should be granted with full compensation and benefits. These are typical parameters, but the contract should be specific. The sabbatical should be planned one year before it is taken and should be continuous, not taken in segments.
- **Mediation.** In the event of conflict or disagreement, a plan should be in place on how to proceed with intervention and reconciliation, if possible.
- **Termination.** This is the process whereby either party may terminate the relationship. Usually a sixty- to ninety-day notice is required.

MUTUAL EXPECTATIONS

One of the biggest conflicts that can arise between a church and its newly called pastor is a gap in expectations between the search committee, the pastor, and the congregation. Understandings about the role of the pastor and his or her duties may be out of sync. This could be due to the search committee negotiating agreements to which the congregation was not privy, or if they had been told, they did not remember. The pastor too may have favorite "hobby horses" or ministries that he likes to ride that may be outside the orbit of the job description or become too much of a priority.

For instance, say the search committee asked the incoming pastor to spend 20 percent of her time in the community, networking, building relationships, and joining community organizations to help bring newcomers into the church. Some members don't know about that priority or don't appreciate it. They want to know why the new pastor is not visiting parishioners and the homebound as much as the previous pastor did. This can result in unrest or criticism.

The best way to prevent this situation is to clearly communicate the call agreement and the rationale behind it to the congregation. Do it with handouts, in the bulletin, from the pulpit, in the newsletter, in committee meetings, and in the weekly e-newsletter if you have one. Ideally, if the pastor is expected to spend that much time in the community, the call would have been built upon a mission or vision statement that included reaching out to the community and growing the church as one of its goals. A search committee can always make an appeal to the mission statement to which the congregation agreed.

SHARED OUTCOMES

In addition to negotiating a fair contract and making sure that mutual expectations are clear and agreed upon, the search committee, with the support of the congregation and the pastor, need to agree on the outcomes they anticipate in their time of ministry together. Too often our churches are on autopilot, expecting the same plans, programs, and projects to go on every year with the same results. As Peter Drucker reminds us, "There is nothing so useless as doing efficiently that which should not be done at all."[2] Some programs just outlive their original purpose and usefulness. If you were to ask a parishioner, "What does your church do?," you'd likely get the answer, "Why, we have worship and coffee hour every Sunday with Sunday school at the same time. All boards and committees meet once a month on a Tuesday night. Bible study is on Wednesday. There is choir practice on Thursday night. The youth go on a mission trip every other year," and so on.

That describes the cycle of annual and ongoing events. An entirely different, but more important question is where do you see your church going? What might your congregation look like in three to five years if you simply did the same things you're doing now? What would it look like if you had a bold set of expectations and outcomes you hope to achieve under the leadership of your new pastor? What if these were some examples of shared outcomes?

- Our church will grow our worship attendance by 10 percent each year for five years. (Who would lead the effort? How would leaders get congregational buy-in? How would the leadership and congregation measure the success?)
- Every member will contribute a financial gift to our annual stewardship drive, and we will grow the participation of regular givers by 5 percent. (Again, how would the official board and stewardship team or other body make this happen? What's the step-by-step plan? Who would drive the process?)
- At least one-third of our worshiping congregation will participate in twenty-four hours of spiritual formation during the church program year. (This could include a Bible study, prayer group, service project, reading or listening to programs to enhance spiritual growth, or many other practices. Who will lead it? What programs might we offer? How do we get buy-in? And so on.)

These are just a few examples of possible expectations. Your church will have its own goals and plans, whether they are building projects, Christian education programs, mission projects, or classes on grief, parenting, and discipleship. The point is, if you and your new pastor have mutually agreed-upon goals to jumpstart your new ministry together, the relationship will be off to a positive start.

It is also imperative that after your new pastor has been with your church for a year the congregation revisits the mission, vision, and goals of the church according to the input and gifts of the new pastor. Dwight Eisenhower said when it comes to preparing for battle, "Plans are useless, but planning is indispensable." While you can't predict the future, you can anticipate it. You and your pastor will have spent a year getting to know one another, discovering your strengths and growth areas together, where the new pastor excels and has passion, and where you can make an impact on those you serve within and outside of the congregation.

SAY A GOOD GOODBYE AND A HEALTHY HELLO

When it is time for the interim leader to say goodbye, it is very important to make sure he or she leaves well. By that I mean, opportunity is given for the interim minister to say goodbye to people with whom he has had significant relationships, finish up projects and programs, and prepare a "survival kit" for the incoming pastor. There is usually a farewell dinner or reception and a ritualization of the departure as mentioned earlier.

Doing a goodbye well is especially important if the previous pastor left under duress because of clergy misconduct or significant conflict. I once served as an interim at a church where their pastor of eleven years walked off in a huff in the middle of a council meeting and never came back. The congregation never had a chance to say goodbye, grieve, or understand the sudden departure. Psychologists call this emotional cutoff, which means there was an abrupt ending to a relationship, a meaningful goodbye was never had, and there was little or no contact after that. The abrupt ending felt like rejection or abandonment. Therefore, it was very important that I said goodbye in a significant way to prepare a good entrance for the incoming pastor.

Ritualizing the departure during worship is a wonderful way to give significance to the leaving. Find ways to give visual and emotional impact to the farewell, as I described when I picked up my walking stick and took it with me after I said the benediction. It can have the same impact as when we "strip the altar" at the end of a Good Friday service. It is a very powerful symbolic gesture.

A good goodbye is extremely important to ensure a healthy hello to the incoming pastor. A clear and meaningful end to the interim ministry without any emotional cutoff or loose ends will help make this happen. The congregation understands that they may no longer rely on the interim minister for pastoral care, and the interim minister promises that he or she will no longer be their pastor because they have new pastoral leadership. This does not mean that the interim pastor may never have contact with the congregation, but that the relationship has changed and boundaries must be respected.

It is equally important for the congregation to roll out the red carpet for the new pastor so that she or he feels like a VIP. Hospitality goes a long way. Ask the pastor how she would like to be introduced to the church and community. A large congregational gathering such as an all-church dinner? Small group dinners? Individual meetings? Home visits? Meeting people casually? It depends upon his or her personality and comfort level in different social situations. Find out how the new pastor would like to have the church update the office. What kind of computer, software, and other equipment might he like or need? This may have been settled during contract negations. Try to strike a balance between being hospitable and being overly attentive. Little niceties like informing her when trash day is, what's the best pizza place or pharmacy, or where to take recyclables are appreciated.

The arrival of a new pastor is an exciting moment in the life of the church and, with the help of your denominational executives, the day of the call meeting and later the installation can be milestones your congregation can celebrate for years to come.

In all of these steps, whether offering counsel on the search process (but *not* about candidates), preparing well for the incoming pastor, and saying goodbye well, the interim minister is a key resource who has been trained in all of these processes. Don't hesitate to ask him or her for their guidance.

Remember: Be kind. Give each other the benefit of the doubt. Your new pastor will probably step on toes without knowing it. The congregation may cross boundaries without realizing it. There will be changes that no one was prepared for. Be patient with each other and with yourselves. God helped you get together and God will help you through the transition.

QUESTIONS FOR REFLECTION AND DISCUSSION

1. Where is there unity in a vision for the future of your church? Where is there disagreement?

2. Where might there be differences within the congregation or among leadership about mutual expectations and shared objections? How might these be resolved before you sign a contract with a new pastor?

3. What needs to be accomplished for the congregation to be ready for new pastoral leadership both spiritually and materially?

4. What small, hospitable gestures would make the new pastor feel welcome and at home?

10

BUILD A CATHEDRAL!

There is an old rabbinical saying that goes, "God created human beings because God loves stories." The practice of ministry is very much about telling stories. The grand Christian story tells it in seven chapters: Creation (when God decided not to be God without us or the universe), Fall (when we shook our fist in God's face and said no thanks or just walked away), Covenant (when God chose a particular, peculiar people called the Jews to be God's own), Cross (when God dove deep into the human predicament and became a human being among us, and overcame evil, death, disease, and every privation of sin by dying on a cross and rising from the dead), Church (when God does the work of redemption, sanctification, and justice through ordinary, flawed, earthbound people like us), and Consummation (when God sews the whole thing up by creating a New Heaven and a New Earth, whatever that may look like.)[1]

The story is woven together with plots, subplots, treachery, heroics, unexpected twists, complex and modest characters, venal and trustworthy people, a direction, and an ending with meaning and purpose. Wondrously, our story is woven up in God's story, who is masterfully weaving all the broken and loose ends into a wonderful tapestry.

I have often said that one of the privileges of pastoral ministry is that I get to hear so many stories from so many people. Folks I thought were ordinary sermon hearers and pew sitters had walked the Appalachian Trail, biked across the entire United States, worked on the Hubble telescope, held her husband in her arms while he died of a heart attack, or raised four happy, healthy children who had made something of themselves. I experience more life in a year vicariously than most people do in a lifetime.

Each congregation has its own Once Upon a Time story. It's their own story of unique origins, peaks and valleys, revered pastors, history-shaping events, bad behavior, and significant ministry that has touched people in their community and around the globe. That story is to be cherished and to be learned from.

Churches, like people, have a worldview or a certain disposition. A worldview is an overall belief system, the grid that orders all of life. It is the disposition or posture by which we interpret our world and our lives, being guided by our theology, upbringing, and life-shaping personal and historical events. A worldview is often a tendency or a default mode. Some churches and people are inherently pessimistic and look at the world through Good Friday lenses, while others take on an optimistic Easter view of life.

A transitional period is a time to remember those stories and unearth any latent worldviews. It is a time to bring forward the lessons and behaviors from when we were at our best and to own and learn from those times when we were not at our best. Looking at our story without rose-colored glasses is just as important as not seeing it through night-vision goggles. It wasn't and isn't always rosy, nor was it or is it always dark. It was deeply human, as people trying to be Christ followers stumbled along the moil and toil of daily life.

The Apostle Paul said, "We have this treasure in jars of clay to show that this all-surpassing power is from God and not from us" (2 Corinthians 4: 7). We carry the treasure of the Gospel—of God's creative, redemptive, sustaining love for us and all of creation—in this deeply flawed humanity of ours.

I have covered a lot of ground in this book. My hope is that it didn't overwhelm you but excited you to all the possibilities of a time of interim ministry. I hope you have gained an understanding of the changing religious landscape in America and some of the ways the church needs to adapt as it does ministry in the twenty-first century. An interim minister could not possibly do everything that is suggested in this book. Together the leaders of the congregation and the interim will prayerfully discern the priorities of their time together and set those as goals. My hope is that this volume will prompt you to think into the near and far future about the work you would like to do to progress as a healthy, faithful, and effective church.

In spite of our flawed humanity, I think the best days of the church lie ahead—that is, if churches are willing to do the hard work of adapting to a new culture and finding a new way of doing church and mission. It will not be easy. Churches tend to be conservative institutions, resisting new or unfamiliar territory. Sometimes it seems the Holy Spirit has to move through twelve committees to get anything done. It's like moving the *Queen Mary* with an oar.

Because churches have these tendencies, having an intentional interim minister or transitional specialist is so strategic. She can help a congregation remember its unique story with all its freckles, pock marks, and dimples. A congregation can rejoice in its successes and repent and learn from its failures. They can reframe certain chapters to look at them differently, in more nuanced ways. A negative story might yield some positive outcomes. By talking, dreaming, and planning, a church can outline some new chapters for the days ahead. People can decide how they want the story to unfold as they go forward.

The assumptions and the plot line of the older story may no longer sustain the church today. An interim pastor can coach a congregation as they navigate those choppy waters. By engaging the five focus points, having important conversations, and experimenting with new ministries, the people can write a new story even as they are living it.

In any story, there are characters—heroes, villains, protagonists, antagonists, ordinary and everyday folks, and complicated figures. All have a unique personality and stories that have shaped them. When you throw them all together in this soup we call "church," it can be a heady mix. My wife says she thinks there is a factory somewhere that manufactures church people and distributes them across the country. Every church has the bosomy lady with big hats who hugs everyone until they pop. There are the bean counters who want to understand every jot and tittle in the budget. There's crazy Uncle Charlie who's always the life of the party.

Writing a "family story" is an important piece of a time of transition. Just as our families have photo albums or scrapbooks, or an elder member of the family might keep genealogies and diaries and write family histories, so each congregation has a story that needs to be told. This story should ring true to active participants even if portions of it make them cringe or confront them with a harsh reality. At this point, the congregation can decide what the next chapters are that need to be written and what they might look like. In a worst-case scenario, a congregation may decide that it's time to write the last chapter. Regardless, the tragedy would be to let the manuscript lie unfinished because the group didn't have the courage or energy to conclude the plot.

Behind all stories is God. God has a story and God has a dream. From the outset we see in the creation story that God decided not to be God without us. To be sure, God does not need us in order to be God. God existed in blessed self-existence for eternity before the universe or human beings showed up. God had a dream and shared that dream with Abram and Sarai: "I will be your God and you will be my people."

In the biblical story we often see God working behind the scenes, pulling levers, raising and lowering curtains, whispering lines to actors who have forgotten them. Before God raised up Moses to lead Israel from Egyptian slavery, there were two Egyptian midwives, Shiphrah and Puah, who pulled Moses floating in a basket from the Nile. Pharaoh had ordered that all Hebrew baby boys were to be killed because he was alarmed at the rate they were reproducing and would soon overpopulate Egypt. The baby was given to Pharaoh's daughter to raise and Moses's mother to nurse. So where was God in the midst of the cries for liberation coming from the Hebrew slaves? God was in the lovemaking of those slaves, at the birthing stools of the midwives, and in all the daily activities of the Hebrew women. In back of it all was God, fulfilling the promise given to Abraham in Genesis 12:2, "I will make of you a mighty nation . . . your descendants will be like the sand on the seashore."

Or remember the Joseph story where his brothers sold him to slave traders on their way to Egypt? The next time they saw him he was the righthand man of Pharaoh, handing out grain to the masses who were starving due to a mammoth famine in the region. When his brothers discovered it was Joseph, whom they betrayed decades earlier, they feared a nasty retribution. But what did Joseph tell them? *"Fear not! What you meant for evil, God meant for good"* (Genesis 5:20). Even in the cruelty of human treachery, God's purposes prevail. Oftentimes we only see God's providential care in hindsight, if at all, but the promise is that God's dream goes on.

God is pulling all of creation forward to a new future, a dream of a new heaven and a new earth, where God will be all in all, where every tear will be dried, every injustice satisfied, every disease healed, where rivers will run clear, creation will live in perfect balance, and death will be no more (Isaiah 65:17–25; Revelation 21:1–4). We don't know what it will look like or when it will happen, but the sure word is that God will write the final chapter and that chapter will have a glorious ending. Even as you and I bear the slings and arrows that life brings, we can live in confidence that in the midst of all the changes and transitions of this life, God is faithful and can be trusted.

Christopher Wren was the architect who designed and oversaw the construction of St. Paul's Cathedral in London for thirty-six years. In spite of setbacks—including its near total destruction by the Great Fire of London, disputes about design and funding from clerics, Parliament, and the City of London—it was completed in 1711. There is a story that Wren was walking among the stonecutters while the cathedral was being constructed. He was curious to know about the magnanimity of the project. He asked one, "What are you doing?" The cutter replied, "I'm hammering this stupid rock." Wren moved along and asked a second stone mason what he was doing. He said, "I'm shaping this rock to be a cornice over a doorway." He finally asked a third, "What are you doing?" Without a moment's hesitation the stonecutter said, "I am building a cathedral!"

Whether you are part of a small rural church, a large downtown church, a struggling ethnic church, or a mega church, and whatever your denomination, theological heritage, accomplishments, or history, always remember that you are part of something far greater than yourselves establishing the reign of God in your corner of the world. Remind yourselves that you are not just bringing a meal to someone who just lost their beloved, leading a small group Bible study, writing a check to fulfill your pledge, or swinging a hammer at a Habitat for Humanity build. You are building a cathedral.

QUESTIONS FOR REFLECTION AND DISCUSSION

1. What is the storyline of your congregation? What are some of the next chapters you would like to write?
2. Do you ever think of yourselves as building a cathedral even as you are involved in the "nuts and bolts" of church life?

3. Appendix G has a comprehensive list of questions for leaders and members of a congregation to reflect upon. Perhaps you might take one section at a time and reflect upon it as an exercise before a board meeting. You might pick the questions or sections you would like to explore with an interim minister.

APPENDIX A

A Behavioral Covenant

As Christians and members of the Valley Community Church, we have been called to live as Christ's disciples and to follow the Golden Rule in dealing with one another. As leaders and as a congregation we wish to model Christ-like love and behavior even in times of discord or disagreement. Therefore, as kindred in Christ we promise to abide by this covenant.

- We promise to express kindness, appreciation, and gratitude to one another for work well done.
- We will be as honest as we can with each other, "speaking the truth in love" (Ephesians 4: 15) and practicing Jesus's teaching by going directly to the person with whom we have an issue (Ephesians 4: 13; Matthew 18: 16).
- We will speak to one another with respect.
- We will all be responsible for the successful implementation of any action we decide to take.
- We will communicate directly to each other using the first person, "I."
- We will speak only for ourselves, not for others.
- We will recognize and identify the merit in another person's idea before we note its weakness or disagree with it.

- We will repeat what the other person has said to confirm we have understood them, and ask them to do the same if we feel we have not been understood.
- We will not jump to conclusions.
- We will listen to understand, but we don't necessarily have to agree.
- We will deal only with verifiable data, not rumors and hearsay, and will seek to understand all sides.
- We promise to pray regularly for one another and to support each other.

(This is but one example of many models and templates for a behavioral covenant. If you do an online search you will find many other examples.)

APPENDIX B

The Mission of First Community Church

We believe that Jesus calls us to love one another, serve our neighbor, and nurture God's spirit within us.

THE CORE VALUES OF FIRST COMMUNITY CHURCH

Personal and Spiritual Growth

We are a church that values personal and spiritual growth in Christ found in worship, adult education opportunities, retreats, and small groups. We desire to grow deeper in our prayer life and our knowledge of scripture so that we may come to know Christ and continue our faith journeys.

(Romans 12: 1–2; Acts 2: 42–47; Matthew 6: 33; Colossians 2: 6–7)

Love

We are a church that values love in our relationship with God, within our community, and for our neighbor. We understand that love is a verb and while we may not feel affectionate or magnanimous toward another, we will always treat them with dignity, respect, and kindness.

(John 15: 9–13; 1 John 4: 7–12; Colossians 3: 12–14)

Community

We are a church that values being a family of faith. We value respectful communication, tolerance of diversity, our intergenerational character, and caring for one another in times of joy and sorrow.

(John 17: 11; Ephesians 2: 13–14; Philippians 2: 4–5; Colossians 3: 12–16)

Mission

We are a church that values opportunities to help others, locally and globally, with their practical needs, as well as bringing others to Christ. We recognize that what we say and do may speak louder than our words.

(John 17: 18; Matthew 28: 18–20; James 2: 15–17; Mark 15: 16; Matthew 25: 40)

We recognize that these are lofty ideals and we often do not measure up to them in a way that would honor the Christ we profess. Nevertheless, we constantly hold them before us as our call to faithful discipleship, being quick to ask forgiveness when we fail and rejoicing in our call to be a faithful community of Christ.

(1 Corinthians 4: 7; Galatians 2: 20)

APPENDIX C

Gut Check: Twenty-Five Key Questions to Measure Church Vitality

Sometimes questions are more important than answers. The following is a collection of questions that vibrant, mission-oriented churches tend to ask themselves on a regular basis. These questions are meant to start conversations, not wars. It is strongly recommended that the church develops a behavioral covenant prior to asking these questions. Churches need to be equipped to have conversations that are civil, compassionate, and Christ honoring. (For more on a behavioral covenant, please read *Behavioral Covenants in Congregations* by Gil Rendle.[1] A sample covenant can be found appendix A.)

The first three questions are applications of Jesus's parable on the talents (Matthew 25: 14–30).

1. How are we becoming a church that God can entrust with even more responsibility?
2. How do we use what Jesus has given us right now and multiply it for the glory of God and for the good of our neighbor?
3. In what ways have we played it safe?
4. How do we view and handle conflict that will inevitably arise due to various differences we bring to the table? What are the unwritten rules in our church and what happens to the people who defy conventionality for the sake of mission?

5. What needs to die in order for us to live? What programs or ideas were effective in the past but are now limiting the health and growth of our congregation?

6. Do we see the church as a safe haven from change or as a change agent in the world?

7. Does our church view the changing culture as a problem to be solved or as an opportunity to be had?

8. How has the community around our church changed in the last five years and how have we changed or not changed with it? What must we learn and unlearn to be effective missionaries in our own culture?

9. If our church ceased to exist, would the surrounding community weep? Would anyone even notice? Would anyone even care?

10. What is it about our experience with Jesus that our surrounding community cannot live without?

11. Where is the Lord in all of this? What biblical story most closely describes what is happening in our church right now?

12. What are the critical areas in which our church can be more dependent on the spirit of God? As a church, how do we continually challenge ourselves to move forward into God's future?

13. Are the leaders in our church mostly catalyzers or stabilizers or a good mixture of both?

14. What is the difference between "doing" church and "being" church?

15. What is the level of spiritual hunger and thirst in our church?

16. What sins does our church need to repent of?

17. What are the normal and natural ways people come to Christ, grow in Christ, and discover and deploy their spiritual gifts?

18. Do I believe God's best blessings are before us or behind us? Why or why not?

19. Do I trust what my friends would experience at one of our worship services? Do I feel confident inviting my friends to church? Why or why not?

20. Do the people believe in the leaders and do the leaders believe in the people? What evidence is there of this one way or the other?

21. What are the living and giving stories from our history—and how can we build on the past without getting stuck in the past?

22. When is the last time someone gave their life to Christ through the ministry of our church? Am I developing any relationships with people who are far from God?
23. When is the last time someone said, "We've never done it that way before?"
24. Why are new programs not always the answer?
25. What is the level of our congregational harmony and transparency to even ask and answer these kinds of questions in a truthful and gracious manner?

APPENDIX D

Sample Interim Ministry Covenant-Contract

Between _____ and Rev. _____ for the purpose of providing interim pastoral leadership during a period of rediscovery and adjustment to change. It is agreed that Rev. _____ will begin service as the Interim Pastor of _____ on _____.

It is understood that the (leadership body) and the Interim Pastor will review this Covenant-Contract at least every six months. It is agreed that this Covenant-Contract shall be in effect for twelve months or until sixty days following a call being extended to a new pastor, whichever comes first, after which time it can be renegotiated up to the time the new pastor starts. Twenty-four months shall be considered maximum time for the interim period unless extenuating circumstances require an extension agreeable to both parties in consultation with the [judicatory official]. Thirty days' notice shall be given in writing by either party of intention to decline an extension. Should either the Interim Pastor or the church wish to terminate this agreement, sixty days' written notice shall be given.

During the interim time the pastor and congregation will, in covenant with one another and with the help of God, seek to

- Provide worship experiences and the practice of ministry with the congregation and community.

- Engage in congregational self-study and goal setting by reviewing the past and planning for the future in such a way as to strengthen and enhance the mission and unity of this church.
- Prepare for the ministry of a new pastor who will be duly called by the congregation.
- Work on the five focus points of congregations in the interim period:

  - Heritage
  - Leadership
  - Mission
  - Connections
  - Future

- Work on any other issues and goals necessary during the interim time as discerned by the transition team and other leaders of the church.

The Interim Minister offers the congregation a rich variety of possibilities to engage these five themes or focus points. Knowing that each situation is unique, the intentional interim strives to discern the tools most appropriate for the specific situations that might emerge. Reflecting upon the five themes or focus points helps a congregation to answer three important questions: "Who are we?" (identity), "Who are our neighbors?" (mission), and "What is God calling us to do and to be?" (vision).

It is agreed that under no circumstances may the Interim Minister be a candidate for the position of called pastor. The Interim Minister will not allow his or her name to be submitted as a candidate nor will members of the congregation ask that this be done. Upon termination and departure as pastor, the Interim Minister will sever his pastoral relations with this congregation, recognizing that all future pastoral functions should be fulfilled by his successor.

It is further agreed that the Interim Minister will not assist the Pastoral Search Committee in the selection of a pastoral candidate. It may be helpful, at times, for the Interim Minister to advise the committee in terms of process, but this may be done only in consultation with and agreement of the conference staff person resourcing the search process and the chair of the Search Committee.

OUR SHARED EXPECTATIONS

The pastoral and professional leadership provided by Rev. _____ will amount to full time or approximately 40 to 50 hours per week. Occasionally, exigencies, such as funerals, a family crisis, or a congregational emergency, do happen that will require the Interim Minister to exceed this average. In those cases, he should be given compensatory time off within a reasonable time after incurring this extra time. Should additional time be needed to provide pastoral services, the matter will be reviewed by the _____, and either the members of the church will assist with the pastoral duties or additional compensation will be offered to the Interim Minister for the additional time.

The Interim Minister will be responsible to the congregation at large, and specifically to the _____.

Pastoral services shall include [the following are examples of what might be included]

- Leading Sunday morning worship and Sunday evening as appropriate, administration of the sacraments including baptism and communion, as well as funerals, weddings, and special services as needed.
- Counseling in crisis situations and referral.
- Serving as lead teacher and resource for the confirmation program.
- Teaching/leading of occasional adult education programs.
- Visiting hospitalized, ill, and other members of the parish needing pastoral care.
- Visiting newcomers and providing newcomer classes with the _____.
- Attending and resourcing meetings of church boards and committees.
- Providing leadership and training for members regarding congregational self-study, future planning, outreach, and stewardship.
- Providing administrative oversight for the daily affairs of the church, including being head of staff, supervising them in the exercise of their responsibilities and ministries for which they will be accountable to the Interim Minister.

- Remaining active in the name of this church in the judicatory region, and the national setting of the [denomination].
- Participating on behalf of this church in ecumenical and interfaith activities in this community.

The congregation will support and cooperate with the Interim Minister in every way and will assume responsibility for

- Regular attendance at worship and meetings.
- Continued financial support for the church and its mission and ministries.
- Support of the Interim Minister in the ministry of this church to the community.
- Sustained lay leadership and shared ministry.
- Establishment of a transition team of five to nine persons agreed upon by the Interim Minister and the [leadership body] whose purpose will be to serve as a confidential support and advisory group for the Interim Minister, to monitor the progress of the accomplishment of interim focus points, and to act as a communication link between the Interim Minister and the congregation.
- Participation in the affairs of the [local and regional denominational settings of the denomination].
- Provision of administrative and secretarial support services, office equipment, supplies, telephone, postage, and so forth.
- Provision of a discretionary fund for pastoral care.
- Keeping the Interim Minister informed of the timing of the transitional leadership, including candidate Sundays and contract termination.
- Participation in a quarterly discussion and mutual review of the total ministry of the congregation, in order to

  - Provide the Interim Minister, the [leadership team], and the Transition Team opportunity to assess how well they are fulfilling their responsibilities to each other and to the ministries they share.
  - Evaluate progress on the focus points and establish and adjust goals for the work of the congregation during the interim time.

- Isolate any goals, areas of conflict, or other matters that have not received adequate attention and may be adversely affecting mutual ministry.
- Clarify expectations of all parties to help put any differences or future conflicts in manageable form.
- Plan healthy closure for the interim ministry by having an exit interview and preparing for the coming of the next pastor.

The _____ of _____ agrees to provide the following compensation to the interim pastor:

- *Base salary.* (According to denominational guidelines. Compensation and benefits for interim pastors should be at least equal to that of the settled pastor.)
- *Housing allowance.* (1 percent of median price of a home in the community the pastor lives in, per month. This is negotiable on the formula your denomination uses.)
- *Social Security offset.* (7.65 percent of cash salary.)
- *Health and dental insurance* for pastor and family/partner.
- *Annuity payment.* (Whatever the formula for your denomination.)
- *Payment of Oxford Criminal Background Check* (if required).
- *Professional development fund* for continuing education, books, and materials needed for ministry. Unexpended funds may be carried over to the next year (includes clergy groups, conferences, workshops, books, and material needed for ministry).
- *An expense allowance* (up to _____ amount annually) for reimbursement of expenses incurred in the course of professional activities on behalf of the church.

Total _____

The Interim Minister is expected to preserve two days a week solely for personal and family use. The Interim Minister is expected to take the time to develop and maintain a healthy physical and spiritual life, including regular exercise, personal retreats, reflection days, and weekly and daily time set aside for prayer, scripture study, and meditation. The Interim Minister with have the following periods of leave at full compensation:

1. National holidays, to be taken so as to not interfere with worship or other congregational events.

2. Annual vacation, at the rate of one month per year, consisting of twenty-three workdays, which shall include five Sundays. Vacation time is accrued at a rate of one week for each three months of service.

3. Vacation and holidays may be postponed and accumulated until the conclusion of this appointment. The [leadership] shall be regularly informed of the amount of time due.

4. Professional development leave at the rate of two weeks a year. This will accrue at one week for every six months of service.

5. Other continuing education events, workshops, and training as offered by the denomination or other ministry-related agencies.

6. Sick days. Paid sick time accumulates at a rate of one day per month up to thirty days.

7. Personal/compassionate leave. Five to seven days per year, except where compassion dictates further extension.

In addition, the church will provide a travel allowance in a total amount not to exceed _____ per calendar year. This travel allowance is to consist of the following components:

- *Commuting Mileage*—a flat rate of $_____ per year. (Refer to IRS Publication 463 regarding commuting to temporary work locations for a period of less than one year: http://www.irs.gov/publications/p463/ch04.html.) It is well documented in many interim ministry handbooks that commuting mileage should be treated like other mileage reimbursements for the first 364 days of the contract. If her interim ministry were to last for longer than one year, then the commuting mileage would need to be paid as taxable income.

- *Business Mileage*—reimbursed at the IRS standard mileage rate for business miles driven for trips between the church location and any other location plus out-of-pocket costs of parking, fees, tolls, and so forth.

This letter may be revised only by mutual agreement, except that compensation and expenses revision shall be mutually agreed upon in a separate budget process.

If the Interim Minister and the [leadership] are in disagreement concerning interpretation of this Covenant-Contract, either party may appeal for mediation to the [local judicatory official].

When the Interim Minister's services at the church ends, the trustees will compensate him for any earned but unrealized vacation and leave time. This compensation is to be paid to the Interim Minister in a lump sum check and includes all aspects of the normal compensation paid to the clergy person.

In accepting this agreement, effective_____ [date], we hereby attach our signatures, making this Covenant-Contract binding upon us in accordance with the above outlined terms.

Interim Minister _____ Date _____

For the Church _____ Date _____

Office held _____

For the Denomination _____ Date _____

Office held _____

APPENDIX E

What Do We Have Energy For?

Every board, committee, and group in the church is given a worksheet (see below). First, you are asked to list all the components of the work you do. (For example: A worship committee might list that they recruit ushers, provide communion elements, recruit acolytes, plan worship with the pastor, etc.). Be sure to list individually all the current tasks you do.

Secondly, list everything you ever dreamed of doing. No idea is too crazy. It can be anything you would like to "test" in the congregation. (So, for example, that same worship committee might list "a healing service," or "have an alternative worship service in a café," etc.) Be creative and have fun listing your dreams—you may be surprised who has been dreaming the very same thing!

Please turn your worksheet in to _____ [whatever group is collecting these sheets].

All the sheets will be collated and formatted. These completed sheets will then be handed out to the congregation (see example). There will be two columns. The first will ask people to rate each item from 1 to 5, one being least important and five being most important. The second column will then ask people to specifically declare which items they are willing to pledge their time, talent, and treasure. All forms must be signed.

When the two columns are compared you discover what people think is just a good idea but have no energy for, and what people are really willing to do. This process helps clarify thinking and keeps a church from spending a lot of time and energy on ministries and missions that no one really wants. This process can also help you rid your church life of "sacred cows," programs that are no longer effective and need to end. Have fun!!

Worksheet for Committees, Boards, and Groups

Please list all the components of what you currently do as a group. Be as specific and detailed as possible. Please list all the programs, events, and mission efforts, whatever that you have ever dreamed of doing. Be as creative and bold as you like. No idea is too crazy.

Sample of a Zero-Based Program Page (that would go to the congregation)

Name (of person completing this form; no unsigned forms will be tabulated):

The worksheet that follows is just an example. You can add as many activities or programs as you like that are relevant to your church.

WORSHIP COMMITTEE

Worship Activities	Rank each item below by a numeric scale. 1=least important, 5=most important.	The church ought to be involved in this ministry. Put a check to so indicate.	I will personally be involved through my time, talent, and treasure.
Ushers			
Greeters			
Welcomers			
Lay reader/participant			
Flowers			
Choir			
Bell choir			
Healing service			
Alternative service—folk, jazz, contemplative, rock			
An updated AV system			
Weekly communion			
Drama and interpretive dance			
Blessing of the animals service			
Weekly confession			
More use of the Statement of Faith			
More youth and children leading worship			
Acolytes			

APPENDIX F

It All Depends

Look at the two images below.

On this page, what animal do you see?

On the next page, how many legs does the elephant have?

It's not what you look at that matters; it's what you see. It all depends upon your perspective.

APPENDIX G

Questions for Congregations

Pastor and church consultant Terry Foland has compiled a host of questions from every area of congregational life to explore during an interim time. You can begin pondering these before your interim minister arrives or with him or her after they arrive.

HISTORY AND HERITAGE

- How do we value our past?
- What have we incorporated into our story of being a congregation from our successes and crises and from our failures?
- How did we evolve into our current set of norms and values, which primarily set the boundaries and determine our way of being a faithful community?
- Have we been enriched by or imprisoned by the events of our history?
- When there have been bad experiences, have we had sufficient closure so that we are not limited by our shame about those experiences and our fear of repeat failures?
- How well do we value our past without letting it determine our present and future life together?

CHRISTIAN COMMUNITY

- Who are we as a corporate "body of Christ"?
- What is our culture or ethos?
- What kind of climate do we provide for people when they come together?
- Is there an atmosphere of caring and support?
- Is this a place where people can feel they belong and are accepted, regardless of their current or past circumstances?
- Are all people welcome here?
- Do we present an openness that invites strangers into the community of gatherings?

DISCERNMENT

- How do we seek to be open to God's call to us as a faith community?
- What distinguishes us from any other human organization?
- Do our efforts to worship help us to discern God's word and call to us as faithful disciples?
- How well do we employ our spiritual disciplines of prayer, study of Scripture, meditation, worship, and stewardship?

SHARED VISION

- What is our way of "being the gospel"?
- Do we regularly engage in efforts to rethink our vision of how we fulfill our mission as a faith community?
- Do we regularly collect information from our setting and look to understand the needs of people around us?
- Do we engage in prayer, meditation, and study of Scripture to help us develop our vision?
- How do we determine priorities for using our limited resources?

MAKING DISCIPLES

- How well do we perform the continuing task of helping people grow in their religious life?
- Do we help individuals discover and claim their particular gifts, skills, and talents?
- Do we help them connect with the faith in ways that contribute to the mission and ministries of the faith?
- How well do we prepare our members to engage in conversion efforts with people who are not part of a faith/belief community?

MINISTRIES IN THE COMMUNITY

- What will we accept as our rules and responsibilities to the people who inhabit our geographic space?
- What services do we provide as part of our discernment of what God is calling us to be and do?
- Does our vision include ways in which we can be engaged both corporately and as individual members in mission endeavors?
- How well do we make use of our resources (facilities, wealth, time, and members) to respond to the needs of those in our defined mission area?

WORLDVIEW

- How big is our world going to be?
- How well do we raise awareness of the concerns and needs in the world and of our interdependence and responsibilities?
- Do we offer members opportunities to respond in a variety of ways to the myriad needs in the world?
- Has our vision included concerns that reach beyond our natural day-to-day interactions?

RELATIONSHIPS

- How do we value differences and deal with conflicts in congregational life?
- Do we engage individuals to articulate their own opinions and beliefs and to respect those of others?
- Do we seek to provide ways for people to get their interests and needs cared for without denying others that same privilege?
- Do we intentionally teach ways of framing conflict in win-win rather than win-lose strategies?

FACING DAILY LIFE

- How does the congregation help people in their daily routines of work, family, and community activities?
- Does the congregation help provide moral and ethical codes by which members are expected to relate to others?
- How does the congregation provide guidelines in the areas of health, finances, life transitions, and mundane routines?

STEWARDSHIP

- How do we teach responsible use of resources by individuals and by the community of faith?
- Do we provide help for our members to understand how money and other financial resources are a gift from God?

LEADERSHIP

- How well is the congregation developing mutual support and ministry in a partnership between clergy and laity?
- How do we share authority and responsibility?
- Do we provide effective ways to define relationships and roles?
- How do we work together to fulfill our vision of being a faith community?

CONNECTION TO FAITH COMMUNITY

- How do we both contribute to and receive support from the structures of our larger denomination, or faith family?
- What does our connection to such a family contribute to our sense of identity and mission?

From Terry Foland, "The Marks of a Healthy Church," *Congregations* magazine from the Alban Institute (November/December 2002).

APPENDIX H

Self-Image Assessment for Local Churches

Circle one or more of the words listed below that you feel best describes our church. You may wish to select more than one, but if you do so, it should be a *dominant* characteristic of our church, not a trait that occasionally or incidentally describes us.

ARMY	COMMUNITY	MISSION
BODY	EMBASSY	PEOPLE
BUILDING	EXPEDITIONARY FORCE	PRIESTHOOD
BUSINESS	FAMILY	RETREAT CENTER
CASTLE	HALFWAY HOUSE	SACRAMENT
CLINIC	HERALD	SCHOOL
COLONY	LIFEBOAT	SERVANT
TEAM	HOSPITAL	COMMUNITY CENTER
MIGRANT GROUP	PROPHET	SANCTUARY

In light of your choice(s), answer the following questions:

What sort of environment does it suggest?

What view of the gospel does it suggest?

What is the role of the church member?

What is the role of the minister?

(For example: Suppose you pick Hospital as a dominant image. You might therefore regard the environment around the church or the people who come to the church as sick. The gospel is the healing medicine. Are church members the patients or the healers, or both? Is the minister the only healer or is he or she the chief of surgery who trains the residents?)

Does this picture accurately represent our church? Or is it one that used to describe us?

Is it one that we gladly embrace? Or is it one that we wish had not been given to us?

Adapted from Ray Bakke, *The Urban Christian* (Downers Grove, IL: InterVarsity Press).

APPENDIX I

Appreciative Interview Guide for Congregations

INSTRUCTIONS

1. In pairs, interview one another using the following questions. Be a generous listener. Do not engage in conversation; rather, take turns and conduct an actual interview. If you need more information or clarification about an interviewee's response, ask additional follow-up questions.
2. Use this sheet to record the results of your interview. When your interviews are completed you will present the results to the wider group.
3. Before you conduct the interview take a minute to read the questions and decide how you would personally answer the question and make a mental note of your response. Then proceed with the interviews, paying full attention to the interviewee rather than to your own story.

QUESTIONS

1. Best Experience: Reflect on your entire experience with your congregation. Recall a time when you felt most alive, involved, spiritually touched, or excited about your involvement. Tell me about this memorable experience. Describe the event in detail.

What made it an exciting experience? Who was involved? Describe how you felt. Describe what you did as a result of the experience.

2. Values: Think about what you value about yourself, being a parishioner, your church, and your denomination. Then answer these four questions:

   a. Yourself: Without being humble, what do you value most about yourself—for example, as a human being, or employee, or a friend, parent, citizen, and so on?

   b. Being a parishioner: When do you feel best about being a parishioner at your church? What about yourself as a parishioner do you value?

   c. Your church: What is it about your church that you value? What is the single most important thing that your church has contributed to your life?

   d. Your denomination: What is it about being a member of your denomination that you value? What is the single most important thing that being from your denomination has contributed to your life?

3. Core Value: What do you think is the core value of your church? What values give life to your congregation? What is it that, if it did not exist, would make your church totally different from what it currently is?

4. Three Wishes: If you had three wishes for your church, what would they be?

NOTES

INTRODUCTION

1. William Bridges, *Managing Transitions: Making the Most of Change*, 3rd ed. (Philadelphia: DeCapo Press, 2009), 3.

2. Ibid.

3. See Molly Dale Smith, ed., *Transitional Ministry: A Time of Opportunity* (New York: Church Publishing, 2009), iv–ix, where Loren Mead gives a more complete history.

1. IT'S NOT YOUR PARENTS' CHURCH ANYMORE

1. Michael Hotit, Andrew Greeley, and Melissa Wilde, "Demographics of Mainline Decline: Birth Dearth," *The Christian Century* 122, no. 20 (October 4, 2005): 24–27.

2. Robert Bellah, "Civil Religion in America," *Dædalus* 96, no. 1 (Winter 1967): 1–21.

3. Will Herberg, *Protestant-Catholic-Jew* (Garden City: NY: Doubleday Anchor, 1960); Diana Eck, *A New Religious America: How a "Christian Country" Has Become the World's Most Religiously Diverse Nation* (New York: HarperCollins Publishers, 2001).

4. Pew Research Center, Religion and Public Life, "U.S. Muslims Concerned about Their Place in Society, but Continue to Believe in the American Dream," July 26, 2017, http://www.pewforum.org/2017/07/26/demographic-portrait-of-muslim-americans/ (3.45 million Muslims); Table of Statistics of the

Episcopal Church, from 2015 Parochial Reports. *Source*: The Office of the General Convention as of January 2017, https://www.episcopalchurch.org/files/table_of_statistics_english_2015.pdf (1.9 million Episcopalians); United Church of Christ Statistical Profile—Fall 2017, The Center for Analytics, Research and Data (United Church of Christ, 880,000 members).

5. The World Bank, Data, population total, Nigeria, https://data.worldbank.org/indicator/SP.POP.TOTL?locations=NG; The World Bank, Migration and Remittances Data, November 16, 2017, http://www.worldbank.org/en/topic/migrationremittancesdiasporaissues/brief/migration-remittances-data; Suburban Stats.org, Miami Dade County, 2017–2018, https://suburbanstats.org/population/florida/how-many-people-live-in-miami-dade-county (1.6 million Latino); World Population Review, "Population of Cities in Cuba (2018)," http://worldpopulationreview.com/countries/cuba-population/cities/ (2.1 million in Havana).

6. Jim Norman, "Americans' Confidence in Institutions Stays Low," Gallup News, June 13, 2016, http://news.gallup.com/poll/192581/americans-confidence-institutions-stays-low.aspx.

7. Pew Research Center, Religion and Public Life, "'Nones' on the Rise," October 9, 2012, http://www.pewforum.org/2012/10/09/nones-on-the-rise/.

8. Pew Research Center, Religion and Public Life, "Religious Landscape Study, http://www.pewforum.org/religious-landscape-study/.

9. Pew Forum, *U.S. Religious Landscape Survey*, June 2008, http://www.pewforum.org/2008/06/01/u-s-religious-landscape-survey-religious-beliefs-and-practices/. In 2017, Public Religion Research Institute found that number to be 24 percent. https://www.prri.org/research/religiosity-and-spirituality-in-america/.

10. Elizabeth Drescher, "Quitting Religion But Not the Practice of Prayer," Religion Dispatches, USC Annenberg, March 28, 2013, http://www.religiondispatches.org/archive/atheologies/6973/quitting_religion__but_not_the_practice_of_prayer/.

11. Robert Putnam and David Campbell, *American Grace* (New York: Simon & Schuster, 2010), 91–133.

12. Peter Kreeft, *Jesus-Shock* (South Bend, IN: Saint Augustine's Press, 2008), 55.

13. Lovett H. Weems Jr., *Changes Congregations Are Facing Today* (Washington, DC: Lewis Center for Church Leadership, Wesley Theological Seminary, 2014), 14.

14. Peter Drucker, "The Five Most Important Questions," http://visionroom.com/sums/Sums-The-Five-Most-Important-Questions.pdf.

15. Anthony B. Robinson, *Transforming Congregational Culture* (Grand Rapids, MI: Eerdmans, 2003).

16. Ibid.

17. John Dorhauer, *Beyond Resistance: The Institutional Church Meets the Postmodern World* (Chicago: Exploration Press, 2015), 63–66.

2. WHAT IS INTERIM MINISTRY?

1. For a comprehensive overview of the work and ministry of the Interim Ministry Network go to http://www.imnedu.org.

2. Norman B. Bendroth, ed. *Transitional Ministry Today: Successful Strategies for Pastors and Churches* (Lanham, MD: Rowman & Littlefield, 2014).

3. William Bridges, *Managing Transitions: Making the Most of Change*, 3rd ed. (Philadelphia: DeCapo Press, 2009).

4. Edwin H. Friedman, *Generation to Generation: Family Process in Church and Synagogue* (New York: Guilford Press, 1985).

5. Salvador Minuchin, an Argentinian family therapist, developed structural family therapy. *Families and Family Therapy* (Cambridge, MA: Harvard University Press, 1974), http://www.minuchincenter.org/.

6. Kenneth A. Halstead, *From Stuck to Unstuck: Overcoming Congregational Impasse*, Alban Institute, 1998. Chapter 8: "The MRI Brief Therapy Skills" lays out a good set of practices and interventions using structural family therapy to help congregations get unstuck.

7. Jay Haley, http://www.jay-haley-on-therapy.com/html/strategic_therapy.html.

8. See Kay Collier McLaughlin, *Becoming the Transformative Church: Beyond Sacred Cows, Fantasies, and Fears* (New York: Morehouse Publishing Company, 2013). See the forward for a list of many congregational norms that should be challenged.

9. Monks of the New Skete, *How to Be Your Dogs Best Friend: A Training Manual for Dog Owners* (New York: Little, Brown and Co., 2001).

3. WHY DO WE NEED AN INTERIM MINISTER?

1. Gil Rendle and Alice Mann, *Holy Conversations: Strategic Planning as a Spiritual Practice for Congregations* (Herndon, VA: Alban Institute, 2003).

2. See Tom Bandy, *Moving Off the Map: A Field Guide to Changing the Congregation* (Nashville: Abingdon Press, 1998) for chapters and exercises on core values and bedrock beliefs.

3. From a document written by Don Remick, associate conference minister of the Massachusetts Conference of the United Church of Christ, called "The Transforming and Transformed Church of the Emerging Era: Characteristics of a Vital Church." Remick drew on many sources of church growth, renewal, and vitality literature and it is used to educate churches about the changing religious landscape in America.

4. Gil Rendle, *Behavioral Covenants in Congregations: A Handbook for Honoring Differences* (Herndon, VA: Alban Institute, 1999).

5. Edwin H. Friedman, *Generation to Generation: Family Process in Church and Synagogue* (New York: Guilford Press, 1985).

6. Anthony B. Robinson, *Transforming Congregational Culture* (Grand Rapids, MI: Eerdmans, 2003).

4. WHO SHOULD WE HIRE?

1. Paul Nickerson, *Assessing Pastoral Candidates*, Evangelism and Congregational Vitality Commission of the Massachusetts Conference of the United Church of Christ.

2. "The Costs of a Bad Hire Can Be Surprisingly High," April 25, 2017, https://www.roberthalf.com/blog/evaluating-job-candidates/the-cost-of-a-bad-hire-can-be-surprisingly-high.

3. Chally Group, "Best Practices in Preventing Leadership Derailment," http://chally.com/best-practices-in-preventing-leadership-derailment/.

4. See Rev. Dr. Rob Voyle's website, Clergy Leadership Institute for a host of resources on appreciative inquiry, http://www.clergyleadership.com.

5. Interim Ministry Network workbook, *The Fundamentals of Transitional Ministry: The Work of the Leader,* appendix 27 and 28.

6. Ibid., appendix 27.

7. Ibid., appendix 28.

5. WHAT WILL WE DO?

1. For detailed information, go to their website https://holycowconsulting.blog/.

2. Additional information is available at their website http://hirr.hartsem.edu/leadership/church_inventory.html.

3. Thomas G. Bandy, *Moving Off the Map: A Field Guide to Changing the Congregation* (Nashville: Abingdon Press, 1998), 163–77.

4. Carl S. Dudley and Sally S. Johnson, *Energizing the Congregation: Images that Shape Your Church's Ministry* (Louisville, KY: Westminster/John Knox Press, 1993).

5. Center for Servant Leadership, https://www.greenleaf.org/what-is-servant-leadership/.

6. Kennon L. Callahan, *Twelve Keys to an Effective Church: Strategic Planning for Mission* (San Francisco: Harper and Row Publishers, 1983), 48. See also https://www.sharefaith.com/blog/2014/06/10-traits-effective-church-leaders/ for another helpful list of traits for effective church leaders.

7. Dan Busby, "Conflicts of Interest: How to Avoid Them, How to Deal with Them, Part 2," http://www.churchadminpro.com/Articles/Conflicts%20of%20Interest%20-%20How%20to%20Deal%20With%20Part%202.pdf.

8. For a useful book on best practices for church governance see Don Hotchkiss, *Governance and Ministry: Rethinking Board Leadership* (Lanham, MD: Rowman & Littlefield, 2016). A useful website on good church management practices may be found at https://smartchurchmanagement.com/effective-church-management/.

9. There are a host of websites that explain SMART goals and how to write them. Here is but one example: https://www.smartsheet.com/blog/essential-guide-writing-smart-goals.

10. Gil Rendle and Alice Mann, *Holy Conversations: Strategic Planning as a Spiritual Practice for Congregations* (Lanham, MD: Rowman & Littlefield: 2003), 8–9.

11. Dorothy Bass, *Practicing Our Faith: A Way of Life for a Searching People* (San Francisco: Jossey-Bass 2010); Barbara Brown Taylor, *An Altar in the World: A Geography of Faith* (New York: HarperCollins, 2009), and Richard Foster, *Celebration of Discipline: The Path to Spiritual Growth* (New York: HarperCollins, 1984).

6. BUT WE LIKE THINGS THE WAY THEY ARE

1. Spencer Johnson, *Who Moved My Cheese? An A-Mazing Way to Deal with Change in Your Work and in Your Life* (New York: G. P. Putnam's Sons, 1998).

2. Tom Rainer, *Who Moved My Pulpit? Leading Change in the Church* (Nashville: B & H Publishing Group, 2016), 2–3.

3. Rev. Kathleen C. Rolenz at http://kathleenrolenz.com/transitional-ministry.html.

4. Eric Liu and Nick Hanauer, *The Gardens of Democracy: A New American Story of Citizenship, the Economy, and the Role of Government* (Seattle: Sasquatch Books, 2011), 11. Cited in Norman B. Bendroth, ed., *Transitional Ministry Today: Successful Strategies for Pastors and Churches* (Lanham, MD: Rowman & Littlefield, 2014), 29.

5. David R. Sawyer and Deborah G. Fortel, *Pathmarks to New Church: A Workbook for Leaders of Communities in Search of Innovation* (Louisville, KY: Flourishing Church Consulting and Coaching, 2015), 15. www.flourishingchurch.com.

6. Ron Heifetz, leadership expert at Harvard business school, uses the "view from the balcony" concept to illustrate an important role of the leader. See Ron Heifetz, *Leadership without Easy Answers* (Cambridge, MA: Harvard University Press, 1994).

7. SHEPHERD, COACH, CONSULTANT, OR CHEERLEADER?

1. Quoted in David M. Atkinson, *Leadership—By the Book* (Dyer, IN: Grace and Glory Publications, 2007), 58.

2. Roger S. Nicholson, ed., *Temporary Shepherds: A Congregational Handbook for Interim Ministry* (Herndon, VA: Alban Institute, 1998).

3. Lovett Weems Jr., *Right Questions for Church Leaders,* vol. 2 (Washington, DC: Lewis Center for Church Leadership, Wesley Theological Seminary, 2013), 12.

4. Weems, *Right Questions.*

5. Ibid.

6. Alan D. Klaas and Cheryl C. Klaas, *Flexible, Missional Constitution/Bylaws: In One Day, Not Two Years* (Kansas City, MO: Mission Growth Publishing, 2000).

7. Ibid.

8. Terry Foland, *IBT* 9, no. 1 (September 1996), 3; cited in *Intentional Interim Ministry Manual*, Committee on Ministry Congregational Transitions Commission, National Capital Presbytery, 4–5.

9. Terry Foland, "The Marks of a Healthy Church," *Congregations* magazine from the Alban Institute (November/December 2002).

8. LIKE A SHARK: MOVE FORWARD OR DIE

1. Quoted in Scott Horton, "Pelikan on Tradition and Traditionalism," *Harper's Magazine*, December 5, 2017, https://harpers.org/blog/2008/12/pelikan-on-tradition-and-traditionalism/.

2. Diana Butler Bass, *The Practicing Congregation: Imaging a New Old Church, Christianity for the Rest of Us: How the Neighborhood Church Is Transforming the Faith* (New York: HarperCollins, 2006).

3. George Bullard, "The Life Cycle and Stages of Congregational Development," http://sed-efca.org/wp-content/uploads/2008/08/stages_of_church_life_bullard.pdf; and *The Congregational Life Cycle Assessment* (Atlanta: Chalice Press, 2013).

4. Mary Sellon, Dan Smith, and Gail Grossman, *Redeveloping the Congregation: A How-to for Lasting Change* (Herndon, VA: Alban Institute, 2002), x–xv.

5. Ron Heifetz, *Leadership without Easy Answers* (Cambridge, MA: Harvard University Press, 1994), 22.

6. Ibid.

7. For a helpful article on applying Heifetz's model to churches, see "Becoming an Adaptive Leader," http://www.faithformationlearningexchange.net/uploads/5/2/4/6/5246709/becoming_an_adaptive_leader.pdf.

8. "Technical Problems vs. Adaptive Challenges," https://www.sgaumc.org/files/files_library/technical_vs_adaptive_challenges.pdf, which was adapted from Ronald A. Heifetz and Donald L. Laurie, "The Work of Leadership," *Harvard Business Review*, January-February 1997, and Ronald A. Heifetz and Marty Linsky, *Leadership on the Line* (Boston, MA: Harvard Business School Press, 2002).

9. Michael Lewis, *Moneyball* (New York: W.W. Norton and Company, 2003).

10. For a good nutshell summary of appreciate inquiry go to "Appreciative Inquiry," Winnipeg Regional Health Authority, 2013, http://www.wrha.mb.ca/staff/collaborativecare/files/AppreciativeInquiry2013.pdf.

9. READY, SET, GO . . .

1. "Difference Between Covenant and Contract," March 29, 2015, http://www.differencebetween.com/difference-between-covenant-and-vs-contract/.

2. Peter Drucker, BrainyQuote.com, accessed December 7, 2017, https://www.brainyquote.com/quotes/peter_drucker_105338.

10. BUILD A CATHEDRAL!

1. See Gabriel Fackre, *The Christian Story* (Grand Rapids: Eerdmans, 1985).

APPENDIX C

1. Gil Rendle, *Behavioral Covenants in Congregations: A Handbook for Honoring Differences* (Herndon, VA: Alban Institute, 1999).

SELECTED BIBLIOGRAPHY

UNDERSTANDING APPRECIATIVE INQUIRY

Branson, Mark Lau. *Memories, Hopes and Conversations: Appreciative Inquiry and Congregational Change*. Herndon, VA: Alban Institute, 2004.

UNDERSTANDING CHANGE AND TRANSITION

Bridges, William. *Managing Transitions: Making the Most of Change,* 3rd ed. Philadelphia: DeCapo Press, 2009.

UNDERSTANDING CHANGING CULTURE

Bass, Diana Butler. *Christianity after Religion: The End of Church and the Birth of a New Spiritual Awakening*. New York: HarperCollins, 2012.
———. *Christianity for the Rest of Us: How the Neighborhood Church Is Transforming the Faith*. New York: Harper Collins, 2007.
———. *The Practicing Congregation: Imagining a New Old Church*. Herndon, VA: Alban Institute, 2004.
Tickle, Phyllis. *Emergence Christianity: What It Is, Where It Is Going, and Why It Matters*. Grand Rapids, MI: Baker Books, 2012.
———. *The Great Emergence: How Christianity Is Changing and Why*. Grand Rapids, MI: Baker Books, 2008.

UNDERSTANDING CONGREGATIONAL CULTURE

Callahan, Kennon L. *Twelve Keys to an Effective Church: Strategic Planning for Mission*. San Francisco: Harper and Row Publishers, 1983.

Halstead, Kenneth A. *From Stuck to Unstuck: Overcoming Congregational Impasse.* Alban Institute, 1998.

McLaughlin, Kay Collier. *Becoming the Transformative Church: Beyond Sacred Cows, Fantasies, and Fears.* New York: Morehouse Publishing Company, 2013.

Oswald, Roy M., and Robert E. Friedrich, Jr. *Discerning Your Congregation's Future: A Strategic and Spiritual Approach.* Herndon, VA: Alban, 1996.

Rendle, Gil, and Alice Mann. *Holy Conversations: Strategic Planning as a Spiritual Practice for Congregations.* Herndon, VA: Alban Institute, 2003.

Robinson, Anthony B. *Changing the Conversation: A Third Way for Congregations.* Grand Rapids, MI: Eerdmans, 2008.

———. *Transforming Congregational Culture.* Grand Rapids, MI: Eerdmans, 2003.

UNDERSTANDING HOW YOUR CHURCH FAMILY WORKS

Friedman, Edwin H. *Generation to Generation: Family Process in Church and Synagogue.* New York: Guildford Press, 1985.

Galindo, Israel. *Perspectives on Congregational Leadership: Applying Systems Thinking for Effective Leadership.* Richmond, VA: Educational Consultants. 2009.

Haley, Jay. *Uncommon Therapy: The Psychiatric Techniques of Milton H. Erickson, M.D.* New York: W.W. Norton and Company, Inc, 1986. http://www.jay-haley-on-therapy.com/html/strategic_therapy.html.

Halstead, Kenneth A. *From Stuck to Unstuck: Overcoming Congregational Impasse.* Herndon, VA: Alban Institute, 1998. Chapter 8: The MRI Brief Therapy Skills lays out a good set of practices and interventions using structural family therapy to help congregations get unstuck.

Johnson, Spencer. *Who Moved My Cheese? An A-Mazing Way to Deal with Change in Your Work and in Your Life.* New York: G. P. Putnam's Sons, 1998.

Minuchin, Salvador. *Families and Family Therapy.* Cambridge, MA: Harvard University Press, 1974.

Steinke, Peter L. *Healthy Congregations: A Systems Approach.* Herndon, VA: Alban, 1996.

———. *How Your Church Family Works: Understanding Congregations as Emotional Systems.* Herndon, VA: Alban Institute, 2006.

UNDERSTANDING LEADERSHIP

Heifetz, Ronald A. *Leadership without Easy Answers.* Boston: Belknap/Harvard University Press, 1994.

Hotchkiss, Dan. *Governance and Ministry: Rethinking Board Leadership.* Herndon, VA: Alban Institute, 2009.

Rendle, Gil. *Behavioral Covenants in Congregations: A Handbook for Honoring Differences.* Herndon, VA: Alban Institute, 1999.

Steinke, Peter. *Congregational Leadership in Anxious Times: Being Calm and Courageous No Matter What.* Herndon, VA: Alban Institute, 2006.

UNDERSTANDING STEWARDSHIP

Christopher, J. Clif. *Not Your Parents' Offering Plate: A New Vision for Financial Stewardship.* Nashville: Abingdon Press, 2010.

————. *Whose Offering Plate Is It? New Strategies for Financial Stewardship*. Nashville: Abingdon Press, 2010.

Durall, Michael. *Creating Congregations of Generous People*. Herndon, VA: Alban Institute, 1999.

Marcuson, Margaret. *Money and Your Ministry: Balance the Books While Keeping Your Balance*. Portland, OR: Marcuson Leadership Circle, 2014.

UNDERSTANDING TRANSITIONAL MINISTRY

Bendroth, Norman B., ed. *Transitional Ministry Today: Successful Strategies for Pastors and Churches*, Lanham, MD: Rowman & Littlefield, 2014.

Durall, Michael. *Don't Wait Until the Pastor Leaves: Planning for Ministerial Transition Helps Ensure That One Successful Minister Follows Another*. Golden, CO: Common-Wealth Consulting Group, 2015.

————. *Like Dating, Only Worse: Rethinking the Ministerial Search Process*. Golden, CO: CommonWealth Consulting Group, 2013.

Mead, Loren. *A Change of Pastors . . . and How It Affects Change in the Congregation*. Herndon, VA: Alban Institute, 2005.

Nicholson, Roger S., ed. *Temporary Shepherds: A Congregational Handbook for Interim Ministry*. Herndon, VA: Alban Institute, 1998.

Oswald, Roy M., James M. Heath, and Ann W. Heath. *Beginning Ministry Together: The Alban Institute Handbook for Clergy Transitions*. Herndon, VA: Alban Institute, 2003.

Smith, Molly Dale, ed. *Transitional Ministry: A Time of Opportunity*. New York: Church Publishing, 2009.

INDEX

mileage expenses, 138
ministry. *See* interim ministry; new
   ministers
MissionInsite, 54
mission of church, 19–22; changing
   notions of, 20; church property as
   place for, 22; collaborative character
   of, 20; congregational growth through,
   22, 24, 58; direct giving as means of,
   22; as essential to church identity,
   26–27, 29, 54, 57, 62, 91; hands-on, 20;
   as interim ministry focus point, 91–95;
   levels of, 93; local nature of, 20; macro,
   93; method, 93, 95; micro, 93;
   partnerships and networks for, 21;
   purpose statements and, 91–92; self-
   image as influence on, 86–87;
   statements of, 92–93; vision statements
   and, 94–95
mission statements, 92–93
modernity, 15
Moneyball (movie), 129
Monks of New Skete, 45
morality, 17
Morgan, G. Campbell, 119
Moses, 7, 43, 116, 148
mutual ministry review, 138
Myers-Briggs Type Indicator, 48–49

Nehemiah, 116
neighborhood/community, of church, 54,
   59, 96, 175
new ministers, 18, 35, 140–141, 142
Nicholson, Roger S., 110
Nickerson, Paul, 68
Nicodemus, 26
nominating committees, 90
Nouwen, Henri, 79

objectives, of churches, 95
office support, 138
Oldsmobile, 9

parental leave, 136
Parish Profile Inventory, 84
partner, of interim minister. *See* spouse/
   partner, of interim minister
Pastoral Search Inventory, 84

pastoral search process: complicating
   factors in, 48; interim ministers'
   relation to, 65; time required for, 37,
   47; and welcoming of new pastor, 142
Paul, Saint, 3, 16, 19, 26, 63, 79, 97, 98,
   116, 146
Pelikan, Jaroslav, 122
pensions, 137
Percept, 54
personal days, 136
personal growth. *See* Christian formation;
   churchgoers: personal transformation
   of
personal qualities and characteristics, 70,
   75–76
personnel manuals, 90
perspective taking, 171, 171–172, 172
Peter, Saint, 7
pilgrim churches, 87
pillar churches, 86
Pine Ridge Reservation, South Dakota, 20
plans, for church congregations, 95
Pledge of Allegiance, 11
policies and procedures, 89
postmodernity, 15–17, 31
prayer, 58, 68, 69, 98
Presbyterian Church, USA, 74
problems: appreciative approach to,
   129–131, 181–182; technical vs.
   adaptive, 127–129
Professional Transitional Specialists
   (PTSs), 74
prophet churches, 86
Protestantism, 10, 23, 27, 77
Proverbs, 69
pulpits, 103
purpose statements, 91–92
Putnam, Robert, 17

questions, for congregations, 107,
   111–113, 119, 155–157, 173–177

Rainer, Thom, *Who Moved My Pulpit?*,
   103
redevelopment, 126
reference checks, 71, 77
relationships: in church life, 61, 73, 91,
   123, 124, 176; with community, 59; as
   focus point, 96; as integral to mission,

ABOUT THE AUTHOR

Norman B. Bendroth is a professional transitional specialist trained by the Interim Ministry Network and serves on their faculty. He has served as a settled pastor in two United Church of Christ congregations and as an interim minister in ten others. He is the author of *Transitional Ministry Today: Successful Strategies for Churches and Pastors* and has contributed articles to *Christian Century*, *Congregations*, *Sojourners*, and more. He is also a board-certified coach and church consultant.

Bendroth is the director of Wicked Awesome Church Consulting (http://www.church-consultants.org/) and is available for coaching and consulting with local churches, nonprofits, and judicatories.